LESSONS

from a

DREAM
MAKER

TEN PROVEN STEPS THAT WILL TURN YOUR DREAMS INTO REALITY

JOE LAND *with*
BILL PERKINS

ACKNOWLEDGMENTS

Hidden behind every book are numerous people who made the book a possibility. Nobody deserves more recognition than my wife, Lynn. She is an ongoing source of inspiration as well as encouragement that never seems to run dry. Lynn, thank you for persevering with me during the days when one business dream died and another was born.

Of course, I would never have found the strength to press on without my daughters, Mary Courtney, Meredith, and Lauren. I thank each of you for inspiring me to stand up and fight again for our family.

I don't believe I would have seen any of my dreams come true without the help of my mentors. My father-in-law and friend, Ben Josselson, mentored me in business. Thank you, Ben, for giving me the opportunity to succeed in business. I also want to thank Bobby Richardson, the former New York Yankee great and coach at U.S.C. Thanks, Bobby, for teaching me how to walk by faith. I also want to thank my business mentor and friend, Bubba Pratt. I can never thank you enough for believing in me when I did not believe in myself.

And of course, my friend Bill Perkins. Without you this dream would not be possible. Thank you for pulling this book out of me and for making this project a success.

There are countless others who have inspired me along the way. Thank you for your willingness to share yourself with me and with others. I've tried to acknowledge the source of the many stories and anecdotes I've used in this book and apologize for anyone I may have unintentionally failed to acknowledge.

I'm expecially grateful to God for making my dreams come true.

TABLE OF CONTENTS

THROW CAUTION TO THE WIND AND DREAM BIG!

Dream makers know that tomorrow's success is built on today's dreams.

One day my wife, Lynn, and I were talking about an idea I had that would significantly expand our trucking business. As we talked, my two older daughters entered the room, sat comfortably on the two ends of a couch, and listened attentively.

"Daddy's a dreamer," Mary Courtney said.

I shrugged my shoulders and smiled.

"Yes," Meredith, my middle daughter, interjected, "but Daddy's dreams *always* come true."

The moment she uttered those words I had an unexpected insight. It seemed like she had slipped a lost puzzle piece into the middle of a picture, and suddenly the image made sense.

I'm not a dreamer; I'm a dream maker.

7

You may read that statement and wonder what exactly makes someone a dream maker. I've defined a dream maker as a person with transferable techniques that enable him or her to bring bodacious dreams into reality. Several things about that definition are important.

First, the techniques of a dream maker are transferable. I believe dream making is an art, like playing the piano, with techniques that can be studied, practiced, and mastered.

Second, dream makers know how to bring seemingly unrealistic dreams into reality.

These two truths are significant because their effect on your life can be profound. They will encourage you to open the cage and release your God-given dream so you can begin making it come true.

EVERYONE'S A DREAMER—EVEN YOU!

Webster tells us a dreamer is a person who has bold ideas or plans—a visionary.[1] It only takes a moment's reflection to realize that every major scientific and social breakthrough flowed from somebody's dream. Lee Eisenberg, a contributing editor to *Esquire* magazine, wrote concerning nine visionaries: "While their contemporaries groped at the present to feel a pulse, or considered the past to discern the course that led to the moment, these nine squinted through the veil of the future. Not that they were mystics.... For the most of them, reality was pure and simple. What set them apart was the conviction that a

While dreaming comes naturally, dream building must be learned.

greater reality lay a number of years down the pike."[2]

Dreaming big isn't a practice utilized only by the men and women whose ideas shape the course of human history. Everyone is a dreamer—including you. Indeed, you were born to dream just as you were born to breathe. Think about it for a moment; as a child didn't you dream about playing in the World Series, competing in the Olympics, or appearing in the movies?

Did anyone sit down and teach you how to dream like that? Of course not! You weren't taught how to dream; you were taught how *not* to dream. Why? Because dreamers are viewed as unrealistic and impractical. Over the years, well-intentioned teachers, parents, and friends convinced you that it's not prudent to be seen as "unrealistic" or "impractical." Eventually, you jettisoned your dreams like unwanted cargo.

A problem is nothing more than the difference between what you have and what you dream about having.

Yet, I'm convinced that dreaming is as essential to your emotional well-being and success as breathing is to your physical health. Caged in the recesses of your imagination is a bodacious dream waiting to get out. It's pleading with you to give it your full attention so it can be translated into reality. And something deep inside of you knows that the realization of your God-given destiny depends on your willingness to unleash that dream and pull together the resources needed to build it into reality.

Of course, you're reluctant to give the dream your full

attention because you don't know what to do with it. But the dream, like a persistent child, won't go away. Will it? You're not alone in your struggle. In fact, the difficulty you face is as common as the common cold. In a single sentence, here's the problem:

While dreaming comes naturally, dream building must be learned.

The gap between dreaming and dream building has to be bridged, or your dreams will remain on the other side of reality, just beyond your grasp. What you need are lessons from a dream builder that will encourage you to dream big and then help you to translate those dreams into reality.

WHAT WOULD YOU DO IF?

When you dream, forget about time and financial limitations. Dreams know no boundaries except those set by your imagination. If God has given you a dream, then He will also give you the resources needed to bring it into reality. Ask yourself: "What would I do with my life if time and money were not a problem?" Remember that a problem is nothing more than the difference between what you have and what you dream about having. Until you articulate the dream, you can't assemble the resources needed to solve the problem.

DON'T SIT AROUND

I love the true story of Larry Walters. As a former trucking executive I've met some interesting truck drivers, but I've never met one like Larry Walters. He was a truck driver who refused to let disappointment destroy his dream.

Larry's lifelong vision was to fly. When he graduated from high school, he joined the Air Force, but poor eyesight disqualified him from pilot school. He eventually left the Air Force and became a truck driver. When he wasn't working, Larry would often sit in a lawn chair in his backyard and watch jets streak across the sky overhead.

One day he got tired of watching others fly and decided to do something about it. He visited a local army-navy surplus store and bought a tank of helium and forty-five weather balloons. Yes, you read it right—he bought *weather* balloons, not party balloons. These heavy-duty spheres measured more than four feet across when inflated.

Once he had all of the materials, Larry returned home and attached the balloons to a lawn chair he had anchored to the bumper of his Jeep. He inflated the balloons and loaded his chair with sandwiches, soft drinks, and a BB gun—which he figured he'd use to pop a few of the balloons when it was time to return to earth.

Satisfied with his preparations, Larry climbed into the chair and cut the cord. He had calculated that the balloons would slowly lift the chair into the air, enabling him to float just over the tops of the houses in his neighborhood. Can you imagine his surprise when the chair shot into the air, leaving under him houses, trees, buildings, and even clouds? He climbed and climbed until he leveled off—are you ready for this—at eleven thousand feet!

It didn't take long for Larry to realize that shooting out a few balloons might unbalance the load, spilling more than the sandwiches and soft drinks. So Larry Walters floated around at eleven thousand feet for fourteen hours.

Eventually, he drifted into the approach corridor for Los Angeles International Airport, and a Pan Am pilot radioed the tower.

"Pan Am Flight 204 to the tower."

"Copy," the tower said. "Go ahead."

"I'd like to report the sighting of a man in a lawn chair with a gun across his lap floating at eleven thousand feet."

As evening approached, the wind currents pushed Larry out to sea. At that point, the Navy dispatched a helicopter to rescue him. But the rescue team failed because the draft from their propeller kept pushing him farther away from the coast. Eventually, they positioned the helicopter over Larry and dropped him a rescue line, which they used to lower him back to earth.

As soon as he climbed out of the lawn chair/hot-air balloon contraption, the police snapped a pair of handcuffs on Larry's wrists. As he approached the squad car a television reporter called out, "Mr. Walters, why'd you do it?" Larry stopped, eyed the man, then replied nonchalantly, "A man can't just sit around."[3]

Like Larry Walters, dream makers don't just sit around—they make things happen. And making things happen begins by throwing caution to the wind and dreaming big.

BIG-LEAGUE DREAMS

As a boy I dreamed of becoming a major-league baseball player. I know most kids foster similar dreams, but my dad convinced me that even my wildest dreams could come true. Although Dad had only a fifth-grade education and worked as a master mechanic in a textile mill, he was exceptionally intelligent and athletic. And he was devoted to me. Every day he'd come home after putting in twelve hours at the mill and play catch with me in the backyard

Day after day we'd play ball together—I'd pitch and he'd catch. He'd position himself in front of the garage and use an old board as home plate. I had a small fielder's glove, and he used a catcher's mitt.

"You can really throw that ball," he'd say. "You've got a lot of heat."

When I started playing Little League, Dad actually built a pitcher's mound in the backyard. Every day after practice I'd walk into the house convinced that no kid in America could throw like me. And every night I'd fall asleep dreaming of playing in the big leagues.

One day, during my junior year of high school, I threw a fastball as hard as I could. My dad caught the ball, stood up, threw his catcher's mitt on the ground, and shaking his left hand said, "I can't play catch with you anymore."

Afraid I had done something wrong, I asked him why not. "You throw the ball so fast I can't see it coming," he said with a broad smile lighting his face.

After that, he took an old paintbrush and painted a target on the side of the garage. He gave me a bag of baseballs, and every day he watched as I hurled pitches at that target.

"You'll be a professional ballplayer some day. I guarantee it!" he said.

Of course, nobody in our small town had ever played a professional sport. Periodically someone would remind me of that. "What makes you think you'll ever make it in the big league?" they'd ask.

In 1966, when I was eighteen years old, I received a letter from the Dodgers. I tore open the envelope, unfolded the single page of stationary, and read the words. A professional baseball team had drafted me! Overnight, the same people who had questioned my dream said, "I knew you could do it."

One of the happiest moments of my life occurred when Leon Hamilton, the chief scout for the Dodgers, visited my house. As the two of us talked, my dad sat a few feet away and listened. The dream we had nurtured had finally come true.

Of course, you realize that there are millions of kids who dream of becoming a professional athlete, but they lack the physical strength or speed needed to play at that level. Maybe you had such dreams yourself. And after realizing they couldn't be realized, you decided to dream more realistically. Or you stopped dreaming altogether.

Dream makers don't stop dreaming just because they suffer a setback.

I know how it feels to fail. Instead of playing for the Los Angeles Dodgers, I accepted a scholarship to play for the University of South Carolina. The plan was to get three years of my education finished and sign at the end of my junior year. God had a different plan. During a close game my junior year, I overworked my arm and tore my rotator cuff—ending my baseball career.

But dream makers don't stop dreaming just because they suffer a setback—I'll talk about that more in Lesson 7. Instead, I dreamed of building one of the largest trucking companies in the country. Twenty-three years after I started the company I had two thousand employees, fifteen hundred trucks, and the tenth largest refrigerated trucking company in the United States.

TURN YOUR DREAM LOOSE

When an unexpected change in the marketplace forced me to sell the company, I replaced that dream with an even more bodacious dream that is now becoming a reality.

Lesson number one from the dream maker is for you to throw caution to the wind and dream big. Refuse to allow failures in the past or fears of the future to restrict the size of your dream. Throwing caution to the wind when you dream isn't so easy because, as I mentioned earlier, you may have been taught how *not* to dream. Since that's possible, I want to help you relearn what you instinctively did as a child—I want to help you dream big.

Unleash Your Passion

As a boy I dreamed of playing professional baseball because I loved the game. And because I loved baseball, I loved to practice. If you're doing what you're passionate about, you'll enjoy the journey as much as the destination. In fact, if you're doing what you're passionate about, work will be fun. When I quit playing baseball, I dreamed of building a national trucking company because I loved competing against other entrepreneurs. Today I'm building an e-commerce business because I'm passionate about helping others succeed.

If you want to identify your passion, analyze your daydreams. When you lie in bed at night, what do you dream about before you fall asleep? What would it take for you to leap out of bed in the morning excited about your day? Forget how unrealistic such dreams may be. Forget about your inability to make the dreams come true. Tap into your passion and turn it loose, because your passion will become the stuff of which your dreams are made. Once you've discovered your passion you'll be ready to take the next step.

Regardless of your education, family background, or business success, you can and should be dreaming something so far-fetched it has the potential to blow the world wide open.

Identify Your Purpose

Take some time and imagine you're a spectator at your own funeral—I know it's a ghoulish thought, but do it anyway. Listen to the words of your family and friends as they talk about you. Pay attention to how you're remembered.

Do you like what you hear? Is everybody talking about how you knew why you were here? Are they impressed with how successfully you fulfilled your purpose? Or do their words reveal a life lived without meaning? If you don't like how you think people will remember you, it may mean you don't feel your life matters. You may question whether or not you've accomplished anything of significance.

Now I want you to place the tips of the fingers of your left hand on the inside of your right wrist just below your thumb. If the fingertips are positioned properly, you can feel your pulse. That's great news, because it means you're still alive. And if you're alive, it's not too late for you to identify your unique purpose for living and the bodacious dream that will enable you to fulfill that purpose.

Of course, it may be that the pulse test you just performed only proves that dreamless corpses can still be the residence of beating hearts. Please, don't be like the man whose gravestone read: "Died, age twenty. Buried, age sixty." Regardless of your education, family background, or business success—you can and should be dreaming something so far-fetched it has the potential to blow the world wide open. Consider the facts about this one man:

- At age seventy-nine he invented bifocals.
- At age forty-five he founded an Ivy League university.
- At age forty-three he invented the lightning rod.
- At age forty he harnessed electricity.
- He dreamed of paratroopers from balloons a century before the airplane was invented.
- At age thirty-six he designed a heating stove that's still used today.
- At age thirty-one he founded the U.S. Mail.
- At age twenty-five he founded the first library in the United States.

Benjamin Franklin accomplished all of these feats before he turned eighty-four years old. Equally amazing, he did it with only two years of formal education. How could he accomplish so much? While I'm sure numerous elements contributed to his amazing list of feats, nothing was more important than the fact that he dreamed big. Instead of living a life of quiet desperation, thoughtfully consider what purpose you want your life to fulfill, and then throw caution to the wind and dream about making it happen.

In order to help you focus on your life's purpose, draw a vertical line down the middle of two pieces of eight and a half-by-eleven-inch paper. On the first page label the left column *Likes* and the right one *Dislikes*. Under each label list the attitudes and activities you most like and dislike.

That's the problem with big dreamers— we're stupid enough to imagine the impossible and crazy enough to make it happen.

On the second page label the columns *Strengths* and *Weaknesses,* and list as many under each heading as you can think of.

Once you've taken the steps above, write out *two* purpose statements that utilize your strengths and would be fun to pursue. For instance, my purpose for building a successful e-commerce business is so I can serve, encourage, and bless others. I'm passionate about helping others discover how their dreams can come true.

The next step in narrowing down your purpose statement involves talking with those closest to you. Ask them which of the two statements they think would best utilize your strengths. Pray about each of them. As you do this you'll find one of the purpose statements beginning to capture your imagination. That statement is the one that expresses your life purpose.

As a dream maker I've discovered that writing out my purpose statement is a crucial first step toward making the dream come true. But once you've taken that step, you'll need to take the next one.

Imagine the Details

As a kid I imagined myself in Dodger Stadium in Los Angeles. I could see the faces of my parents and friends in the stands. I could feel the stitches on the baseball and smell the popcorn on the air. I imagined myself striking out the final batter in the World Series.

When I started our trucking business in Florida, I told Lynn, "If we can do it here, we can do it in every state in the country." I imagined offices throughout the country.

When you dream, do it in high-definition color and in stereophonic sound. The greater the details the more compelling the dream will be. Dream makers dream in detail.

Throw Caution to the Wind

I realize there is risk in dreaming big. You could fail. You could look foolish in the eyes of people you respect. You could face repeated setbacks and suffer disappointment.

But consider the fact that making a dream come true begins with a dream. Frankly, I'd rather fail at an attempt to make a bodacious dream come true than succeed at mediocrity. I'm challenged by the words of Mark Sheppard, president of Texas Instruments, when he explained his triumph in the 1970s over industry giants like Westinghouse, GE, and RCA. "Those companies knew all the things that weren't possible," he said. "We didn't. We were stupid."

That's the problem with big dreamers—we're stupid enough to imagine the impossible and crazy enough to make it happen. With that thought in mind, go ahead—throw caution to the wind and dream big. And then turn the page, where you'll discover the next lesson from a dream maker—a lesson that will enable you to bring the realization of your dream one step closer.

DREAM MAKER SUMMARIES

- Throw caution to the wind and dream big.
- Possess transferable techniques that enable them to bring bodacious dreams into reality.
- Ask themselves, "What would I do with my life if money and time were not a problem?"
- Don't sit around waiting for their dreams to come true.
- Enjoy life because they do what they're passionate about doing.
- Have written out a life purpose statement that defines their dream.
- Dream in high-definition color and stereophonic sound.
- Would rather fail at attempting something great than succeed in mediocrity.

Draw a Map
from Where You
Are to Your Dream

*Dream makers know that reaching their dream
requires a map.*

I n *Alice in Wonderland,* when Alice comes to a junction in
the road that leads in different directions, she asks the
Cheshire Cat for advice.

"Cheshire Puss...would you tell me please, which way I
ought to go from here?"

"That depends a good deal on where you want to get to,"
said the Cat.

"I don't much care where..." said Alice.

"Then it doesn't matter which way you go," said the Cat.

That grinning feline spoke the truth, didn't he? If we don't
know where we want to go, then any road will take us there.
Unlike Alice, dream makers know where they want to go.
They're pursuing a blow-your-socks-off vision that has captured

their hearts and minds. But having a dream isn't enough.

When I reflected on why I've successfully made my dreams come true, I discovered I've never been content to just dream. With every vision I've drawn a map from the present to the future I dreamed about. Bringing your dream into reality requires a map...a game plan...a strategy.

I'm convinced that many people never make their dreams come true because they avoid the important process of mapping. Why? Because they don't know how, consider it useless and boring, or they just don't want to put in the effort.

If we don't know where we want to go, then any road will take us there.

If you fit into the category of people I just described, I've got some good news for you. The dream maker system of mapping requires no more than an hour of up-front time followed by regular progress reviews. The process is much like driving somewhere you've never been before. Your first step would be to study a map and chart your course. Once you've done that and embarked on your trip, you'll periodically pause, recheck the map to make sure you're on course, and then resume your journey.

Dream makers know where they're headed. But they also know that without a plan their dream will remain just that—a dream. Making your dream come true demands drawing a map from where you are to where you want to be.

DRAW THE MAP

When I was a boy, my dad never sat me down and said, "Son, let's define your dream." Obviously, that approach wouldn't have worked with me since I was just a boy. Dad did something better; he encouraged me to dream big. He stretched my imagination with images of playing for the Dodgers.

Once he knew the dream was established in my heart, he never said, "Now that we know you want to be a big-league baseball player, let's set some short-term goals." Again, my dad did something better; he came home from work every day and played catch with me. Eventually, I realized that what I did every day would determine whether or not I developed the strength and skill needed to make my dream come true.

Years later I dreamed of building one of the largest trucking companies in the country. Making that dream happen demanded a game plan I had to implement every day. The same is true with my current e-commerce business. It's grown exponentially because I've drawn a map from the present to my dream, and I've followed it diligently.

Write a Description of Your Dream

In lesson 1 I urged you to throw caution to the wind and dream big. I exhorted you to dream in high-definition color and stereophonic sound. Now I want you to take a few minutes to write out a description of your dream. As you do, be sure to record everything that comes to mind. If you tap into your passion and purpose, the experience should be both spontaneous and fun. Once you've done that, take a few minutes and reduce your dream to the bare essentials until you finally have a single sentence or two. My dream, which I've shared with you below, is a summary of a much longer statement that fills in the details.

*To build an e-commerce business that allows me to experience
financial freedom so I can use my success as a platform
to serve, encourage, and bless others.
I don't want to just offer people words of hope;
I want to give them ideas that will so transform their lives
that they become a source of blessing to everyone
who comes in contact with them.*

Notice that I'm not seeking financial prosperity so I can sit around and count my money or play with toys. Financial success is a bridge I had to cross in order to fulfill my passion to encourage others and help them achieve success. It is the platform that enables me to positively affect other lives.

I realize that the first sentence in my dream statement may seem about as exciting as a hospital hallway—cold and antiseptic. But I promise you that when I peel back that single sentence and look behind it—WOW! Behind that sentence are images of my wife, Lynn, and me traveling the world, living debt-free, giving half of our income to God's work, and experiencing the joy of seeing lives transformed by hope. Every time I read my dream statement it stokes my emotional fires and propels me forward through another day.

You're at a crucial juncture in the process of building your dream because you're about to articulate where you want your life to go. And you're about to put in writing a vision that will pull you out of bed in the morning and energize you throughout the day. Take some time and jot down what your dream looks like, and then record a simplified dream statement in the box below.

MY DREAM	DREAM STATEMENT

Now that you know where your life is headed you need to draw a map that will detail the steps needed to get there.

Write out the Steps to Your Dream

When I dreamed of building a trucking company, I knew I had to find funding and acquire trucks, drivers, and customers. Each of those crucial elements required individual steps to bring it into reality. Similarly, when I started my e-commerce business, I needed to educate myself and build strategic relationships. Again, achieving those goals required specific strategies.

It may be that the gap between where you are and where you want to be seems so great that you question whether you'll be able to bridge it. Your dream may appear too lofty. Believe it or not, the following superstars could all identify with you.

Lucille Ball
Bill Cosby
Robert DeNiro
Robert Duvall
Dustin Hoffman
Ronald Reagan
Sylvester Stallone
John Wayne

While not one of them began his or her career with the dream of working as an extra, *that was the first step for each of them.* They had a dream—no doubt about that—but they realized that to bring the dream into reality required beginning where they were and moving on from there.

"God is willing. You've got to be willing."

BUBBA PRATT

Drawing a map to your dream that includes incremental steps, or goals, is important because it helps you to realize that you can achieve your dream. You can, God willing, make it happen. And I might add, as my friend Bubba Pratt once told me, "God is willing. You've got to be willing." I can assure you that when Bubba spoke these words to me, I looked at him and said, "I am willing." And I believe you're willing, too, or you wouldn't be reading this book. Since that's the case, let me tell you how dream makers write and use goals.

AMBITIOUS BUT ACHIEVABLE

Because you've locked on to a blow-your-socks-off dream, you'll need some ambitious goals to enable you to bring the dream into reality. When he was fifteen years old, John Goddard dreamed of climbing every major mountain in the world, exploring the biggest rivers in the world, running a mile in five minutes, and reading the complete works of Shakespeare as well as the entire *Encyclopedia Britannica*. Most people would regard such a dream as nothing more than a childhood fantasy.

Determined to make his dream come true, Goddard wrote three words at the top of a piece of paper, "My Life List." Under the title he recorded 127 specific goals that would enable him to make his dream come true. Most reasonable people would probably consider the list more ambitious than achievable. Yet by 1993 he had accomplished 108 of them. He explored the Nile, Amazon, and Colorado rivers. He studied primitive cultures in the Congo, New Guinea, Brazil, and nine other countries. He climbed Mount Kilimanjaro, Ararat, Rainier, the Matterhorn, and eight other mountains. He became proficient in the use of a plane, motorcycle, tractor, surfboard, rifle, pistol, canoe, microscope, football, basketball, bow and arrow, lariat, and boomerang. He circumnavigated the globe four times and learned French, Spanish, and Arabic. The list of specific goals he accomplished fills four and a half pages of a book.[4]

But remember that John Goddard didn't accomplish those

goals in a day, week, month, or year. He has spent most of his life pursuing the dream—one goal at a time. The next time you find yourself questioning the power of goals to help you realize your dream, just remember the story of John Goddard.

MEASURABLE

Of course, in order to accomplish those lofty goals, Goddard had to decide when he would climb each mountain and explore each river. He had to attach dates to his goals. Dream makers write out goals that are ambitious, achievable, *and* measurable. Again, it's like taking a trip. Once you've found your destination on a map and charted the course, you're careful to identify the places you intend to stop for gas and food. When drawing a map from the present to your dream, you also need to identify specific stopping points—measurable achievements that will serve as emotional fuel and enable you to measure your progress.

These goals may be both personal and professional, but you need to include fun things you want to do or accomplish. I'm convinced that dream makers are men and women who enjoy the journey as much as the destination. And pausing along the way to have fun is a crucial element in pursuing the dream.

In establishing goals, or measurable targets, I've found five years to be a good point of reference. It's enough time to accomplish something significant but not so far in the future to seem unreachable. The process of drawing the map involves asking yourself: "What will I have to accomplish in five years in order to bring my dream into reality?" The answer to that question will provide you with the goals on which you need to focus your attention so you can achieve them. When you add five-year goals to your map, it will look like the three boxes below.

TODAY ⟶ FIVE-YEAR GOALS ⟶ MY DREAM

I realize that the process of listing five-year goals can be as much fun as sitting in a dentist's chair. That's why I never take more than an hour to jot down goals and approximate dates and when I hope to see them realized. Because I believe my best counselors are my wife and three daughters, I include them in the process of goal setting. Some of my goals will never be reached (I have to grit my teeth when I say that because it's hard to admit). Others will be. Dream makers aren't hung up on listing only goals they *know* can be achieved. John Goddard listed as a goal to visit the moon, an ambitious goal he never accomplished—yet. But he wrote it down anyway.

After selling my trucking business, I knew that if I was going to achieve my dream, I'd have to find a business opportunity with tremendous growth potential. With that in mind, I established the following five-year goal:

I want to be financially independent by the year 2000.

When I said I wanted to be financially independent, I meant that I wanted to have enough residual income that I could retire from my traditional job if I wanted to. Actually, my dream was never to retire but to use my success as a platform to help others succeed. But if I spent all of my time running a traditional business, I would be working—not fulfilling my dream. So in order see my vision realized I would need to do something nontraditional to achieve financial independence.

Because it's crucial for you to put your goals in writing, use the space below and write out three five-year goals that must be reached for you to move toward the realization of your dream.

| TODAY | → | FIVE-YEAR GOALS | → | MY DREAM |

Now that you've articulated some five-year goals, you're ready for the next step. Bringing my five-year goal into reality demanded the development of a strategy that consisted of numerous short-term goals. When I incorporated a strategy into my map it took the form shown on page 33.

It's easy when developing a strategy to forget the importance of character. Dream makers know that the makeup of their character will determine the extent of their success. Building a dream on weak character is like building a house on sand—it won't stand. I discovered a long time ago that I must focus as much energy on the development of my inner-person as I do on shaping the world around me. In other words, making my dream come true requires a strategy that develops both my character and my business. That's why my strategy always consists of two parts.

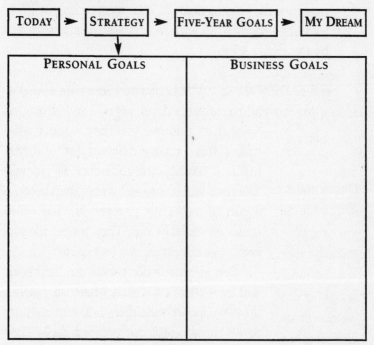

PERSONAL GOALS	BUSINESS GOALS

My list of personal goals consists of over twenty items. These are short-term, measurable steps that must be taken for me to achieve my five-year goal and ultimately the realization of my dream.

My personal goals include:
- reading the Bible and praying daily.
- listening to one positive tape a day.
- reading educational and motivational books for a minimum of fifteen minutes a day.

My business goals include:
- starting a business by June 1996.
- mastering the fundamentals of the business by August 1996.
- forming a partnership with six strategic business leaders by December 1996.

I realize there are scores of books and seminars aimed at helping readers and participants develop goals and strategies. Since that's the case you may wonder what makes this process different for a dream maker. (Actually, the difference is crucial.) The goals and strategies I write down become a part of me. They give me lift, like wind under an eagle's wings. They propel me forward, like the thrust of a jet engine.

Dream makers don't write out their goals and leave them on a shelf where they gather dust. We incorporate them into our calendar so we can monitor our progress daily.

Dream makers don't write out their goals and leave them on a shelf where they gather dust. We incorporate them into our calendar so we can monitor our progress daily. They make up the map we rely on as we move, one day at a time, toward the realization of our dream.

With that thought in mind, take fifteen minutes and write out some short-term goals that you need to accomplish to help you achieve your five-year goals. Be sure to include both personal and business goals. Include some fun goals that will make the journey enjoyable as you realize them. For instance, under personal goals I've listed such things as travel worldwide (that will be fun) and build a pool and cabana at our home. Remember, dream makers like to have fun.

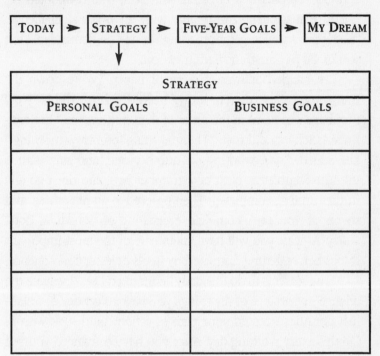

| TODAY | STRATEGY | FIVE-YEAR GOALS | MY DREAM |

STRATEGY	
PERSONAL GOALS	BUSINESS GOALS

THE $25,000 IDEA

After a dream maker has written out a dream statement, identified five-year goals, and developed a strategy, the next step involves translating the strategy goals into a daily action plan. For instance, one of my strategic goals was to form a partnership with six strategic business leaders by December 1996. I transferred that goal onto my daily to-do list by identifying the names of scores of people I needed to call every day in order to identify the leaders with whom I would team up.

You may be familiar with the story about Charles M. Schwab, the president of Bethlehem Steel, who confronted Ivy Lee, a management consultant, with an unusual challenge: "Show me a way to get more things done," he demanded. "If it works, I'll pay anything within reason."

Lee handed Schwab a piece of paper. "Write down the things you have to do tomorrow," he said. Schwab did it. "Now number these items in the order of their importance," Lee continued. Schwab did that. "The first thing tomorrow morning," Lee added, "start working on number one, and stay with it until it's completed. Next take number two, and don't go any further until it's completed. Then proceed to number three, and so on. If you can't complete everything on schedule, don't worry. At least you will have taken care of the most important things before getting distracted by items of lesser consequence.

"The secret is to do this daily," continued Lee. "Evaluate the relative importance of the things you have to get done…establish priorities…record your plan of action…and stick with it. Do this every working day. After you have convinced yourself of the value of this system, have your men try it. Test it as long as you like. Then send me a check for whatever you think the idea is worth."

In a few weeks, Charles Schwab sent Ivy Lee a check for twenty-five thousand dollars. Schwab later said that this lesson was the most profitable one he had ever learned in business.[5]

Like Charles Schwab, dream makers turn their strategic goals into action plans that they diligently put into practice. Every day I check my to-do list, and every day I make sure I accomplish those tasks essential for me to achieve my five-year goals. Dream makers are diligent because the dream that has captured their imagination pulls them forward like iron to a magnet. It compels them to daily achieve what they must in order to make the dream come true.

As you undoubtedly know by now, such diligence requires commitment. If you feel you're lacking in commitment, or if you just need a dose of resolve, then you're ready for Lesson 3.

DREAM MAKER SUMMARIES

- Know where they're headed and have a plan to get there.
- Have goals that are ambitious and achievable.
- Set goals that are measurable.
- Develop a strategy to strengthen their character.
- Develop a strategy to shape the world around them.
- Transfer their goals to daily to-do lists and diligently monitor them.
- Use their goals as a map to direct their lives and monitor their progress.

Don't Tiptoe into the Future... Leap into It!

*Dream makers see an exiting and compelling
future and commit all their resources
to its realization.*

You were designed for commitment just as surely as a ship is built for the open seas and a plane for the sky. If you've never devoted yourself to the realization of your dream, then you're like a clipper ship tethered to a dock or a jet tied down in a hanger. All of your potential is at rest, waiting to be unleashed.

I've learned that making a dream come true demands commitment. Nobody who tiptoes through life, as though he were sneaking through a minefield, will see his dreams realized. Whether building a trucking enterprise or an e-commerce business, I've articulated my dream, drawn a map, counted the cost, and then leaped into the future.

Making your dream come true demands *total* commitment. In fact, I'm convinced that the level of your success will be directly proportional to the level of your commitment. I'm challenged by the words of John Rohn, who said:

> Let others lead small lives,
> *but not you.*
> Let others argue over small things,
> *but not you.*
> Let others cry over small hurts,
> *but not you.*
> Let others leave their future
> in someone else's hands,
> *but not you.*[6]

Dreams aren't like butterflies that will land on your shoulder if you stand still long enough. And you can't wait for someone to place them in your hand. They will only materialize as you work to bring them into being. After examining the specific commitments that have enabled me to become a dream maker, I've identified four that are absolutely essential. As you consider each one it's crucial for you to recognize that many people dream, but only the committed make their dreams come true.

COMMITMENT ONE
I'LL CULTIVATE PRODUCTIVE HABITS

A habit is something you've done so many times that you do it without thinking. Whenever I walk into a dark room, I immediately reach for a light switch on the wall to the right of the door. I do this because experience has taught me that that's where the switch is usually located. I've entered thousands of rooms and reached for thousands of switches. Now I reach for one even if it's not there.

A habit is something you've done so many times that you do it without thinking.

When I'm driving a sports car with a manual transmission, I don't have to think about when to push in the clutch and shift the gears—it has become a habit.

Some habits, like the two I just mentioned, save us time and effort. Others actually interfere with our ability to make our dreams come true. I like to call these habits "ruts." A rut is nothing more than a grave with the ends knocked out. Such ruts include:

- talking instead of listening.
- failing to promptly return phone calls.
- arriving late for appointments.
- refusing to exercise regularly.
- handling mail more than once.
- not paying bills in a timely fashion.
- procrastinating on unpleasant tasks.
- failing to refer to my dream map on a daily basis.
- taking those I love for granted.

When a person develops enough bad habits, his entire life falls into a rut (or, grave) that limits his direction and undermines his potential. He becomes like the truck driver who was hauling a load of cargo across a country road in South Georgia. As he came to a stop sign, the driver of a pickup truck behind him watched in astonishment as the trucker leaped out of the cab of his rig and ran around the trailer banging on it with a baseball bat. When he had completely circled the truck and ruthlessly pounded every side, the driver climbed back into the cab and drove away.

Curious, the driver of the pickup followed the big rig and watched in astonishment as the trucker repeated the process every five miles. When the truck driver finally pulled his rig into a truck stop, the man in the pickup approached him.

Bad habits are like rusted cars without gas. They sit on the streets of our lives, getting in the way.

"Hey, buddy," he said. "I've been following you, and I noticed that every five miles you get out of your truck and run around the trailer banging on it with a baseball bat. I don't mean to be nosy, but why have you been doing that?"

The trucker pushed the brim of his Stetson up with his right index finger, gazed at the man in front of him, and said, "Well, it's this way. I've got a ten-ton truck, and I'm hauling twenty tons of canaries. In order to keep that truck going I've got to keep half those canaries flying."

Often times our lives can become so weighted down with bad habits that we're like that trucker—wasting time on foolish activities that aren't necessary. The solution isn't to scurry around with quick fixes, but to lighten the load on our lives by getting rid of bad habits and replacing them with good ones.

Shedding Bad Habits

The biggest struggle you'll have in breaking a bad habit is overcoming inertia. *Inertia* is a word that describes the fact that an object will remain in a state of rest unless acted upon by something outside of itself. If you've ever pushed a car, you realize that the hardest part of the job is getting the car in motion. Once the vehicle is moving, keeping it going is much easier.

Bad habits are like rusted cars without gas—they sit on the streets of our lives, getting in the way. Moving them will demand energy, but once you've pushed a bad habit out of your life, keeping it away is easier.

The first step involves identifying those bad habits that are holding you back. Review the goals you identified in Lesson 2, and ask yourself if you're doing things currently that will hinder your ability to achieve them. For instance, if you've identified as a personal goal to get in physical condition within six months, then evaluate your current eating and exercise habits. Meeting that goal will demand pushing the rusted car of high-fat and high-carbohydrate foods out of your life. It will mean refusing to continue living a sedentary life.

As you evaluate your life, be ruthless. Don't tolerate attitudes and activities that hold you back. Review the list I mentioned above, and place a mark by the bad habits that characterize your life. Take some additional time, and add a few I haven't mentioned. Once you've done that, prioritize the list. Place at the top the habit you're going to attack first, because it's holding you back the most.

Occasionally I feel compelled to point out a crucial difference between dreamers and dream makers. Dream makers take the matter of getting rid of bad habits and replacing them with good habits very seriously. We don't view bad habits casually because we know our dreams will never become reality if we don't take charge of our lives, push against the bad habits, and get rid of them. But dream makers know it's never enough to shed bad habits; we must replace them with good ones.

Dream makers know that their habits shape their character and their character determines their future.

Cultivating Good Habits

Dream makers cultivate productive habits. Why? Because they know that their habits shape their character and their character determines their future. As I mentioned earlier, the hardest part of breaking a bad habit and starting a new one is overcoming inertia. Researchers say it takes twenty-one days for a behavior to become a habit. That means that if you'll stick with a good habit for just three weeks, you'll find yourself doing it without thinking about it. In fact, I've discovered that once a habit is in place, it's harder *not* to do it than to do it.

Several years ago I realized I had fallen into the rut of taking more from people around me than I gave. That bad habit exhibited itself in the tone of my voice and the demands I placed on my family and friends. I decided to shove that bad habit out of my life and replace it with a better one. My personal goal became to daily tell those closest to me that I loved them. At first those three words felt awkward rolling off my lips. But after a few weeks it became easier. Today it's a habit that has transformed my life and the lives of those I'm closest to.

That's just one example; I could give scores of other bad habits I've shed and replaced with good ones. But the key lesson for you is this: Dream makers commit themselves to cultivating productive habits. Todd Rainesberger once said, "Most people live in a gray area of life between commitment and resignation." Such people never give up, and they never make a lasting commitment. I agree with Todd's exhortation, "Put effort behind your dream."

This is especially important in regard to what we looked at in Lesson 2. You must articulate your dream, map out the goals and strategies necessary to reach it, and regularly refer to your dream map. Are you ready to make a commitment to cultivate such habits? If so, then you're ready for the second commitment, because it flows from the first.

COMMITMENT TWO
I'LL USE MY TIME WISELY

It's startling to consider the fact that time is distributed equally to us all. Whether a politician or paperboy, housewife or executive, rancher or financier, business owner or hourly worker, the clocks we buy all run at the same rate. All of us have exactly the same number of minutes in our hours as everyone else has. Think about it for a moment: *Nobody has more time than you do!* And in the final analysis, time, not money, is the currency of life.

The fact is that no one has control over the speed at which time passes. Ultimately, when we talk about time management, the issue isn't one of controlling our time, but of controlling ourselves. Dream makers know that time is an instrument for measuring how effectively they're developing the attitudes and actions needed to bring their dream into reality. They view time as a tool for evaluating how well they're utilizing their abilities to make their dream happen.

Because your day has exactly twenty-four hours, it's easy to conclude how some of your time should be spent.

- Sleep…approximately eight hours.
- Meals…approximately two hours.
- Shower and dress…approximately half an hour.

I realize you may sleep more or less and take more or less time to shower and dress. But based on these approximations, you have 13.5 hours a day to spend with your family, exercise, educate yourself, work, and relax. Often times urgent activities crowd out important ones. Most people devote attention to problems that make the most noise rather than devoting themselves to those activities that will help bring their dream into reality. Because their lives aren't dream driven, they never even consider how their time could be used more effectively.

Consider the fact that a study done by the Nielsen Company revealed that the average person in the United States watches 6.5 hours of TV a day. That means there are some people who watch more. A person who spends 6.5 hours in front of a television every day will have watched eleven years of TV by the end of his life.

Suppose for a moment that you are way under the average and only watch television for three hours a day. And suppose that you decided to spend one of those hours reading a book or listening to an educational tape. In one year you will have spent 365 hours developing your character. If you divide that by a forty-hour work-week, you'll have added nine and a half additional weeks of learning to your life. That's like spending two and a half months sitting at the feet of the world's greatest dream makers.

While you may not waste much time watching television, chances are you do habitually waste time doing something unproductive. Find out what it is, and utilize part of that time to develop your character or work toward the accomplishment of one of your goals.

Dream makers know that small segments of time every day add up to large chunks of time in a year. The key issue for you is to brutally evaluate how you use your time and cut back on activities that don't help you develop the attitudes and actions needed to bring your dream into reality. Take two days and record, in fifteen minute segments, how you use your time. Once you've done that you'll see where change is needed. Remember that everyone has the same amount of time in a day—dream makers use their time wisely.

COMMITMENT THREE
I'LL MAINTAIN AN OPTIMISTIC ATTITUDE

I love the story about identical twin brothers Richard and Robert. Both had brown eyes and black hair. Both stood four feet six inches tall. Although the boys were identical in appearance, in others ways they were different, even opposite.

It was their ninth birthday, and the twins were excited about the surprise gifts they would receive from their parents. Since they were twins, they would receive identical gifts— ponies. But instead of simply handing over the ponies, the parents decided to show the boys a pile of manure and see if they could guess what they would receive.

To heighten the suspense, the parents blindfolded Richard and led him into the barn, where his gift was hidden. After the blindfold was removed, Richard's face clouded in disbelief. "A barn full of manure!" he said in disgust. "What kind of a present is this? Why did you give it to me? I deserve better."

He dropped his head, kicked the dirt at his feet, and as he trudged away muttered, "What an awful present."

The parents then brought Robert into the barn and took off his blindfold. He immediately grabbed a shovel and started digging. Thrilled beyond belief, he frantically hurled manure into the air.

Shocked by Robert's enthusiasm, his parents asked why he was so excited. Stopping for a moment, the breathless boy exclaimed, "With this much manure, there's got to be a pony in here somewhere."

This story illustrates the difference between a pessimist and an optimist, a person with a negative attitude and one with a positive attitude. Which child are you most like? Do you tend to assume the worst or look on the bright side of everything?

Whenever I stress the importance of an optimistic attitude I always point out that neither optimism nor pessimism defines reality. Instead, each is a perception of reality. Nobody's a pessimist all the time. Most of us have a streak of negativism. That's okay. A touch of pragmatism sometimes prevents us from making foolish decisions.

But a pessimist isn't pragmatic. He views life through a dark lens. The word *negative* comes from the Latin word *negare*, meaning to deny. A negative person is one who constantly tells him- or herself, "I can't; it won't work; it's not good enough." Every time a positive thought tries to emerge, the negative ones drive it right into the ground.

George Burns described a pessimist as "a man who feels bad when he feels good for fear he'll feel worse when he feels better." John Glasworthy observed that a pessimist is a person "who is always building dungeons in the air."

Spouses and children of pessimists are generally filled with anger and resentment. Layers of gloom separate them from the ones they love. Family members eventually rebel against the daily reality of something always being wrong. They tire of the continual barrage of faultfinding, grumbling, murmuring, and complaining. They would like to get through just one day without hearing about poor health, a failing business, bad weather, lost friendships, and other negative aspects of life.

Because pessimism drains emotional energy and undermines relationships, dream makers keep it out of their mental system as though it were poison (which it is!). How do we do that? Just as it's crucial to exercise the body to keep it in shape, so is it important to exercise our minds to get rid of mental fat—and I consider pessimistic attitudes a form mental fat. I could give you a long list of exercises, but we dream makers like to keep things simple. With that in mind, there is a single mental exercise I perform throughout every day to trim away excess pessimism.

Focus on the Positive

It's counterproductive to say to myself, "I won't think negative thoughts. I won't think negative thoughts." That's about as effective as telling myself, "I won't think about white elephants with red spots. I won't think about white elephants with red spots."

By telling myself what I won't think about, I'm actually thinking about it. Whenever I catch myself being pulled into a current of pessimism, I say, "Every obstacle is an opportunity." I then immediately replace the negative thought with a positive one.

I constantly remind the members of my team when they bring up a "problem" that there are not problems, just opportunities.

The other day while driving to Atlanta from Charleston I was caught in a traffic jam just like a fly in a spider web. My immediate reaction was, "Oh man! What lousy luck! I'll be late."

Once I realized "stinkin' thinkin'" had infected my mind and had begun to drain away emotional energy, I said to myself, *Hey, this is a great chance to make some phone calls I hadn't planned on making until this evening.*

Not only do I refuse to focus on the negative, but I also refuse to allow those around me to focus on the negative. I constantly remind members of my team when they bring up a "problem" that there are no problems, just opportunities. If there are alligators snapping at your heels, don't say, "I'm gonna be eaten alive!" Instead say, "I'm gonna make myself a pair of shoes with a matching belt or pocketbook."

As you strive to follow your dream map by implementing your strategy you'll face all sorts of "problems." Dream makers consistently turn those problems into opportunities for growth. They refuse to allow them to create pessimism.

About now you may be saying, "Such optimism is unrealistic. I can't do it." I think you need to know that it's not unrealistic. If you want to become a dream maker, you will do it. And I'm convinced the final commitment you need to make is the one that will enable you to keep the other three.

COMMITMENT FOUR
I'LL CULTIVATE MY FAITH

During the darkest days of my life I watched helplessly as the trucking business I had spent twenty-three years building slowly slipped into a dark abyss. When I retired at age forty-five and handed the business off to one of my best friends to run, I had no idea he would make decisions that would drive the company to the brink of bankruptcy.

One day a manager called and said, "Joe are you coming back to work?"

"I don't think so," I said.

"Well, you've made my decision too. I'm quitting because we won't make it without you."

I had a decision to make. Either let the company go or return, fire my best friend, and right the company. I chose the latter. In a short time I found a company that was $1.2 million out of margin on its bank loan and hemorrhaging to the tune of $300,000 in cash per month.

One day I received a phone call from the bank loan officer assigned to our account. "Joe, I found a way to get your company in margin," he said.

"How's that?" I asked.

"I'm going to bounce your checks until you're there."

I'm a lightbulb, and God is the light socket.

A short time later I received a phone call from an associate, "Joe, you had better look at these checks that the bank is sending back to us."

"What's the problem?" I asked.

"They've got the phrase, 'Refer to Maker,' stamped on the back side."

I want you to know I'm not an unusually mystical person. I'm a businessman. But in that moment I believed that God had used those canceled checks to get my attention. I needed to reconnect with my maker. I hung up the phone and got on my knees right there in my office, because I knew I had wandered away from my faith in God. I had been so successful in everything I had tried that I forgot that I needed Him.

Lord, You are my Maker, I prayed.

When I think about my faith in God, which I express through faith in Jesus, I see Him as the ultimate source of power in my life. I'm like a lightbulb, and God is the light socket. If I'm not connected to God, I haven't got the power to do what He created me to accomplish.

The element of faith is crucial because it is the power of

God that enables a dream maker to keep his other commitments. If you find committing to productive habits, using your time wisely, and maintaining an optimistic attitude seem beyond you, then make the cultivation of your faith a priority. I love the words of Jesus when He said that He is the vine and we are the branches. The key to successful living is to keep connected to God so He can give us His strength.

I began this chapter by noting that you were designed for commitment. The truth is that you'll never see your dreams realized until you stop *thinking* about what you want to do and commit yourself to do it. Dream makers don't tiptoe into the future; they leap into it. And it's time for you to make the jump—review the four commitments I've noted in this chapter and make them. Once you've done that, turn the page because you're ready for Lesson 4.

DREAM MAKER SUMMARIES

- Ruthlessly shed bad habits.
- Diligently cultivate productive habits.
- Manage their lives so that they make the best use of their time.
- Focus on the positive.
- Cultivate their faith in God because they know He is the source of their strength.

Pursue Your Dream with Passion

*Dream makers see the future, and
it fuels their emotional fires.*

There is a fundamental truth of life that every dream makers knows: *People are influenced more by someone's beliefs and emotions than by any amount of logic and knowledge.* This is true because people don't care how much you know until they know how much you care about them and whatever you're pursuing.

Michael LeBoeuf has been called the "most savvy salesman in America." He's written several books and addressed companies all over the world. In one of his books, *How to Win Customers and Keep Them for Life,* he tells a true story aimed at illustrating the importance of enthusiasm.

The Power of Passion

The leading character in the story, famous New York diamond dealer Harry Winston, possessed a precious stone he thought a wealthy Dutch merchant might want to see. As in any business, rumors circulate freely, and Winston had heard that the merchant was searching for a certain kind of diamond to add to his collection.

People are influenced more by someone's beliefs and emotions than by any amount of logic and knowledge.

During an international phone call, Winston described the stone and invited the potential customer to fly to New York and examine it for himself. Excited that his search might be over, the merchant made the flight and took a limousine to a downtown hotel.

In keeping with his business practice, Winston didn't present the stone to the customer himself, but assigned that responsibility to his best salesman, who met the merchant at the entrance of the store. The salesman escorted the customer to a glass case in the rear of the showroom. He quickly unfolded a black velvet cloth, spread it over the surface of a glass countertop, and turned on the small desk lamp that rested immediately beside the cloth. With utmost precision the salesman placed the stone on the velvet cloth and began to point out its technical features. The more he talked, the more unsettled the merchant appeared. Finally, the customer said, "It is a beautiful stone. But not what I'm looking for."

Winston, who had been watching the presentation from across the room, intercepted the merchant at the door and asked, "Since you came all this way to see the stone, would you stay a few minutes more and allow *me* to show you the diamond?"

"Certainly," the Dutch merchant said with a thick accent.

As the two men stood over the diamond Winston spoke spontaneously, not about the technical features of the stone, but about its beauty. He enthusiastically admired the diamond's rare color and brilliance. As he praised the stone the customer tilted his head slightly to the right and smiled. Winston talked about the ceremonious history of the diamond, and the merchant nodded his head, clearly impressed.

Soon, the customer knew he must purchase the stone. It alone would complete his collection.

While waiting for the diamond to be packaged, the Dutch merchant pondered what had just occurred. Curious, he asked Winston, "Why did I buy the diamond from you when I had no difficulty saying no to your salesman?"

Smiling, Winston gave an insightful answer. "That salesman is one of the best men in the business, and he knows more about diamonds than I do. I pay him a good salary for what he knows. But I would gladly pay him twice as much if I could put into him something that I have and he lacks. You see, he *knows* diamonds, but I *love* them."[7]

Passion, like a magnet, will pull people to you and your ideas.

Passion, like a magnet, will pull people to you and your ideas. That's why it's so important for you to pursue your dream with enthusiasm. Cavett Robert, the founder of the National

Speakers Association, captured the essence of this truth. "You *tell* from here," he said, pointing to his head. "But you *sell* from here," he said placing his right index finger over his heart. "The most persuasive person in the world," he continued, "is the one who has a fanatical belief in an idea, a product, or a service. Words can be refused. But a positive attitude that springs from a sincere belief cannot."[8]

Passion is persuasive because it's contagious. Helena Modjeska, a nineteenth-century actress, gained widespread popularity because of her ability to communicate her emotions. She once gave a dramatic reading in Polish (her native tongue) to an English-speaking audience. Helena tapped into her emotions so completely and communicated with such feeling that she had her audience in tears. Only later did the audience discover that the actress had recited the Polish alphabet.[9]

If an actress could move an audience to tears with pure emotion, how much more can you influence people around you if you're passionate about the dream that's captured your heart?

EVERYONE'S PASSIONATE ABOUT SOMETHING

Maybe you're thinking, *But Joe, I'm just not an enthusiastic person.*

I don't buy that. I've watched some passive people tap into a geyser of hand-clapping, high-fiveing, backslapping enthusiasm when their favorite sports team scored a touchdown or a game-winning run. I've seen straight-faced parents leap with excitement when one of their children catches a fly ball in a Little League baseball game or kicks a goal in soccer. I've known single adults who've fallen in love and refuse to stop talking about their romantic interest. And then there's the unbridled enthusiasm of the man or woman who just bought a dog or a new car.

Everybody possesses a reservoir of enthusiasm that's waiting to be tapped. In lesson 1 I urged you to articulate a dream that flowed from your passion and expressed your purpose for living. If you did that then you've probably already noticed that the more you focus on your dream, the more compelling it becomes. Each time you imagine making it a reality you connect with the core of your being, and a dose of emotional energy surfaces. That energy translates into compelling conversation and infectious enthusiasm.

I stay passionate about my dreams by listening to stories about other dream makers who pursued their dreams with passion.

When the Los Angeles Dodgers drafted me, do you think I needed someone to twist my arm and make me talk about it? Of course not! From the first time I slipped my hand into a baseball glove and threw a pitch I wanted to play in the big leagues. I couldn't talk about baseball with passive indifference. I loved the game, and everybody who knew me realized I loved the game. If they didn't want to talk about baseball, they knew they had better not hang around with me. My vision to play in the big leagues flowed from a love for baseball that created an engine of enthusiasm.

Today I'm excited about my e-commerce business because it's the number one shopping mall on the Web and because it provides me with an opportunity to create the kind of wealth needed to make my dream come true. Not only that, it has the potential to accomplish the same thing for everyone on my team. Every day I live with enthusiasm because every day the realization of my dream is one day closer.

HOW TO STAY PASSIONATE, ABOUT YOUR DREAM

Now that you're learning to dream in high-definition color and stereophonic sound it's time for you to discover how dream makers stoke their enthusiasm. I want to warn you that the answer is simple—but it does require effort. I stay passionate about my dream by listening to stories about other dream makers who pursued their dreams with passion.

Jackie Robinson: Passionate about Baseball (My Kind of Man!)

Because I'm a great fan of the American pastime, I want to introduce you to one of baseball's greats. While you probably recognize his name, you may not be aware of how important his passion for baseball was to his success.

In 1947 Jackie Robinson's lifelong dream came true—he became the first African American to play in major-league baseball. I'm convinced it wasn't his exceptional athletic ability that set him apart from others. While athleticism certainly played a major role in his achievement, something more important enabled him to stand out from the crowd. Jackie Robinson had a passion for the game of baseball. He would not rest until he faced a big-league pitcher and chased fly balls in a big-league outfield.

"It won't be easy," Branch Rickey of the Brooklyn Dodgers

told him. "You'll be heckled from the bench. They'll call you every name in the book. The pitchers will throw at your head. They'll make it plain they don't like you, and they'll try to make it so tough that you'll give up and quit." Then he added sternly, "But you won't fight back, either. You'll have to take everything they dish out and never strike back. Do you have the guts to take it?"[10]

Jackie Robinson had the "guts" to endure because he never allowed disappointment or adversity to diminish his passion for a dream others had ridiculed. Jackie Robinson was a dream maker whose passion paid off big time. In 1947 he became the National League Rookie of the Year and in 1949 the Most Valuable Player, eventually entering baseball's Hall of Fame with a lifetime batting average of .311.

Jackie Robinson had the "guts" to endure because he never allowed disappointment or adversity to diminish his passion for a dream others had ridiculed.

King Camp Gillette: Passionate about Disposable Razors

Almost every adult in the United States begins his or her day with a shave—the face for men and the legs for women. Although some Americans use an electric model, the majority of us use a handheld razor. The sharpness and disposability of a razor blade is something we take for granted. But the invention of disposable razors flowed from the passion of a single man with an unusual name: King Camp Gillette.

The idea started as nothing more than a passing thought. But the more he considered the possibility, the more possible the idea seemed. Eventually, the possibility became a passion that King Camp Gillette determined to pursue with tireless energy. All he needed was an engineer, mechanic, or cutler to build him a prototype. Nobody would. Instead, they said his idea was nothing more then a "cockeyed invention." Experienced cutlers, metal workers, and even experts at the Massachusetts Institute of Technology said it couldn't be done. They insisted that nobody could manufacture a razor sharp enough to give a clean, smooth shave and inexpensive enough to be thrown away when cutting facial hair had dulled its edge.

Gillette refused to allow the "stinkin' thinkin'" of others to keep him from energetically continuing his search for financial and engineering help.

The dream had so captured his heart that Gillette refused to allow the "stinkin' thinkin'" of others to keep him from energetically continuing his search for financial and engineering help. Four years after he initially had the idea Gillette finally produced his first disposable blade. You'd think with a blade in hand, so to speak, he would have no trouble getting it on the shelves of stores. It didn't work out that way for King Camp Gillette. Indeed, had it not been for his untiring enthusiasm he would have given up. It took Gillette six years, *after the production of the first blade,* to get the razor on the market. And if he expected to cash in quickly, he would have faced another disappointment. The first year Gillette sold just 52 blades at $5 each—that's less than $300 gross earnings.

Did his enthusiasm and determination pay off? You know

it did. In the second year he sold 90,844 blades and changed the way we shave. He once told *Advertising and Selling* magazine, "If I had been a technically trained engineer, I would have given up."[11]

King Camp Gillette had something more valuable than an education, money, or friends in high places. He possessed a compelling dream and the passion to pursue it in the face of repeated setbacks.

Peggy Flemming: Passionate about Ice Skating

I've got to admit that the next story is for those of you who love ice skating more than baseball. Of course, I realize that Olympic ice skating is one of the most watched athletic events on television. Those of us who have been around more than thirty years know that a single woman with a passion for the ice raised our awareness and love for the sport.

A passion for skating became the fuel that drove her to practice longer and harder than anyone else her age.

In her autobiography, *The Long Program*, Peggy Flemming says she began skating almost by accident. Her mother noticed an advertisement in a local paper for a new rink that offered special introductory prices. She immediately signed up her nine-year-old daughter for lessons. Of course, you can take a child to the ice rink, but you can't make her love to skate. That's something that happened to Peggy the moment she stepped on the ice. Skating was an epiphany for Flemming and served as the single element of life that caused everything else to fall into place.

A passion for skating became the fuel that drove her to practice longer and harder than anyone else her age. In fact, she discovered that the difference between good and great was fifteen minutes. When she was just thirteen, Flemming practiced every day at a local rink from 5 to 7 A.M. with another young skater. But she realized that more time would enable her to improve faster than the other girl. So she entered the deserted rink fifteen minutes early. It's certainly legitimate to wonder if she loved getting up every morning before sunrise. Just for the record, she didn't. And it's also fair to ask if she loved going to the rink every day before school and then returning after school where she practiced until dinner. Again, she didn't love missing out on the activities other kids enjoyed.

Make no mistake about it, Peggy Flemming didn't love losing sleep or playtime. But she did love skating. In fact, she loved it so much she was willing to pay any price to become the best in the world. And her enthusiasm for skating paid off with storybook achievements. Peggy Flemming won the World Figure Skating Championship three times from 1966–1968, the Olympic gold medal in Grenoble, France, in 1968, and five U.S. national championships. Her skill and beauty on the ice inspired a generation of young women to take up the sport.[12] She accomplished that by transforming competitive skating into an art in which she passionately expressed her inner being.

Brian Everett: Passionate about Helping Kids with Cancer

It's easy to think about famous people when identifying dream makers who pursued their vision with passion—people like those whose stories I just told. But sometimes people whose stories are unknown to the general public inspire me. True stories like the one involving Brian Everett.

No parent ever wants to hear a doctor say, "We have a problem." Especially if their ten-year-old son has been complaining of headaches. Or, blacking out.

The news was frightening. "Brian has a brain tumor," the doctor said.

It took a moment for those five words to sink in. And then the physician gave the bad news, "It's malignant. And it's big— a fourth to a third of the size of his brain. If we don't operate immediately, he could be gone in a week." His parents felt as if someone had just grabbed their stomachs and squeezed hard, refusing to let go.

The news didn't upset Brian, a fifth grader, at least not at first. Initially, his parents hid their fear. But they couldn't keep the monster locked up. How can a parent shut the door on their terror and pretend it's not there? How could they ignore the realization that their child might soon slip away from them never to be held or hugged again? When Brian sensed the fear in his parents, he too started to fear.

The more he dreamed, the more passionate he felt about the idea.

Of course, everyone put a good spin on the problem. After all, lots of NBA stars have shaved heads— stars like Air Jordan and Shaq. These are big strong men whose ranks Brian joined when the surgeons shaved his head as smooth as a billiard ball before removing the tumor.

Sleep came faster than Brian could count backwards from 100 to 96.

Eight hours later the surgeon peeled off his rubber surgical gloves. He pulled off his pale blue surgical mask. He slipped out of the powder white surgical gown. And he smiled. It had gone well. Real well. Brian and his parents could relax—the monster turned out to be toothless.

That was ten years ago. Neither chemotherapy nor radiation treatments was necessary because the surgery went so well. And since there was no trace of the cancer, Brian could move on with his life.

But Brian refused to move on without looking back. Several years ago Brian, who is now twenty, dreamed of helping others kids who suffered from cancer. The more he dreamed, the more passionate he felt about the idea. Eventually he decided to help raise money for other kids in tight situations. He joined Kids Making Miracles, a fund-raising organization at Doernbecher Children's Hospital in Portland, Oregon—the hospital where his surgery was performed. Brian believed passionately that he, and his friends, could raise enough money to make a difference. As cochairman of the group Brian set a lofty goal—he intended to raise $1 million.

With a full head of hair, Brian got to join Michael Jordan and Shaq at the NBA All-Star Game in Cleveland. Brian and a handful of other TeamUp kids were honored at the game. Although Brian may never slam-dunk a basketball over Shaq, he did something that required even more courage—he beat cancer and allowed his victory to fuel a personal passion for helping other kids do the same thing.

REMEMBER THIS TRUTH

I opened this chapter by stating that *people are influenced more by someone's beliefs than by any amount of logic and knowledge.* Because dream makers know this principle is true, they pursue their dream with passion. They refuse to allow any degree of disappointment, adversity, or hardship to extinguish the fire that burns in their hearts. Consequently, like a burning log, they ignite the passion of others.

Stoke the fire that burns within you by taking the following steps:

Every morning begin the day by reading your dream statement.
Before sleep review your dream statement, and ask God
to energize you during the night.
Listen to taped messages in which other dream makers
tell their story.
Read inspirational books written by dream makers.
Build friendships with dream makers.

As you pursue your dream you're going to encounter unique opportunities to make it come true. In lesson 5 you'll learn what to do when a strategic opportunity crosses your path.

DREAM MAKER SUMMARIES

- Know that people are influenced more by their beliefs and emotions than logic.
- Know that enthusiasm is contagious.
- Know that everyone has a reservoir of enthusiasm waiting to be tapped.
- Cultivate enthusiasm within themselves by listening to the stories of other dream makers.
- Review their dream every morning and night.
- Build friendships with other dream makers.

WHEN THE TIDE IS HIGH— SET SAIL!

*Dream makers recognize strategic opportunities
and seize them.*

After I graduated from high school, my dad, who only had a fifth-grade education, urged me to go to college before playing professional baseball. "The Dodgers will be there when you graduate," he said. "And you'll be a smarter man and a better pitcher."

Following my dad's advice, I accepted a scholarship to play ball at the University of South Carolina. On the day of my first start I felt like a flock of butterflies had taken up residence in my stomach. After surveying the pitcher's mound, I dug a small hole in front of the rubber with the cleats of my shoes. When I had prepared the mound so it would support my throwing motion, I faced my catcher, All-American Dan Scarper. A moment later I wound up and fired the ball into his glove.

When the umpire sensed I had thrown enough pitches, he barked out a loud command: "Play ball!"

Dan hurled the baseball to second base to start the game. I turned toward third base to get the ball, but it wasn't there. Confused, I looked to first base; it wasn't there either. I then faced home plate and saw Dan walking toward me. Now I want you to know he intimidated me. He stood six feet three inches, grew up in Scarsdale, New York, didn't talk with a Southern drawl, and never ate grits.

An opportunity occurs when the elements needed for your dream to be realized come together at the same time.

Uncertain what he intended to do, I stood on the mound like a puppy dog waiting for its owner to walk in the door. When he reached me, Dan took the ball out of the palm of his catcher's mitt and dropped it into my glove. He gazed into my eyes and said, "Joe, this is the moment you've been waiting for your entire life. This is the opportunity you've trained for your entire life. Give them the heat!"

I took that ball out of my glove and knew that Dan had hit the nail on the head. I was fired up. I made up my mind that I would seize the opportunity with everything in me. And I did. I struck out the first nine batters, and we went on to win the game.

SEIZE THE OPPORTUNITY

Webster tells us that an *opportunity* is a "favorable juncture of circumstances." An opportunity occurs when the elements needed for your dream to be realized come together at the same time—like they did for me on that spring day at U.S.C. And like they will for you. Yet opportunities are as rare as lunar eclipses—they happen, but you've got to look for them.

The great English playwright and poet William Shakespeare described strategic moments that must be grabbed:

> There is a tide in the affairs of men,
> Which, taken at the flood, leads to fortune;
> Omitted, all the voyage of their life
> Is bound in shallows and in miseries:
> And we must take the current when it serves,
> Or lose our ventures.

In the ancient world, ships would enter a harbor at high tide and receive cargo. Once loaded, a heavy vessel couldn't depart until the next high tide. If the captain failed to set sail during the high tide, he would miss the chance to leave port. Similarly, when the tide is high, you must board the ship and begin the voyage. The tide won't wait—and neither will strategic opportunities for you to realize your dream. When the circumstances for success merge, you must act. As an insightful writer once said: *"On the plains of hesitation bleach the bones of countless millions; when given an opportunity, they sat down to contemplate it, and there they died."* Because the realization of your dream will rest upon your ability to seize strategic opportunities that

If someone builds his dream on antiquated ideas, products, and systems of delivery, he'll be doomed to failure.

come your way, I'm going to provide you with five dream-maker principles that will help you do just that.

PRINCIPLE ONE
BUILD THE PRESENT ON THE FUTURE

Dream builders make a habit of studying today's trends so they can anticipate tomorrow's opportunities. That's crucial because if someone builds his dream on antiquated ideas, products, and systems of delivery, he'll be doomed to failure. Over 165 years ago Martin Van Buren wrote a letter to President Jackson. The letter opposed the changes that new railroads would introduce to the United States. Historians debate the authenticity of the letter, but its tone reveals a man who wanted to anchor tomorrow's opportunities on the past.

January 31, 1829
To: President Jackson:

The canal system of this country is being threatened by the spread of a new form of transportation known as "railroads." The federal government must preserve the canals for the following reasons:

One. If canal boats are supplanted by "railroads," serious unemployment will result. Captains, cooks, drivers, hostlers, repairmen, and lock tenders will be left without means of livelihood, not to mention the numerous farmers now employed in growing hay for horses.

Two. Boat builders would suffer, and towline, whip, and harness makers would be left destitute.

Three. Canal boats are absolutely essential to the defense of the United States. In the event of the expected trouble with England, the Erie Canal would be the only means by which we could ever move the supplies so vital to waging modern war.

As you may well know, Mr. President, "railroad" carriages are pulled at the enormous speed of fifteen miles per hour by "engines" which, in addition to endangering life and limb of passengers, roar and snort their way through the countryside, setting fire to crops, scaring the livestock, and frightening our women and children. The Almighty certainly never intended that people should travel at such breakneck speed.

Martin Van Buren
Governor of New York

I can't keep from chuckling when I read that letter, because I know that Van Buren meant what he said. He had become so linked to the past that he refused to imagine a future where canals would be replaced by railroads. Dream makers never allow their knowledge of the past to prevent them from seizing present opportunities. They know that present dreams must be built on future opportunities. With that knowledge, they apply the next principle.

PRINCIPLE TWO
STAY OPEN TO UNEXPECTED OPPORTUNITIES

Several years ago my nephew Faust Chitty and his wife, Sandy, asked if they could meet with Lynn and me about a business opportunity. Of course, he was a young entrepreneur, and I was the founder of a trucking company. I could think of plenty of reasons *not* to meet with him—like, "He's my nephew!"—but a long time ago I made a commitment to remain open to unexpected opportunities.

Dream makers never allow their knowledge of the past to prevent them from seizing present opportunities.

With that in mind I agreed to a meeting, and the two of them came over. When I opened the door of our Charleston home and saw Faust dressed in a suit and tie, I said to myself, *I don't know what he's doing, but he sure means business.*

Over the next hour they shared with us a strategy to create residual income through an e-commerce business. I found their ideas intriguing, but before agreeing to go into business with Faust, I wanted to do two things. First, I wanted more information about the future of e-commerce. Second, I wanted to meet someone who had successfully built a similar business. Dream makers know that the only way to determine if an idea is strategic is to check it out.

PRINCIPLE THREE
STUDY AN OPPORTUNITY TO SEE
IF IT'S STRATEGIC

Not only did I have my financial advisers check out the company Faust had told me about (they came back with an A++ rating and high recommendation), but I also showed due diligence and researched the future of e-commerce.

Martin Van Buren failed to realize that commerce would be

conducted differently in the future than it had been in the past. He was like the naysayers who said that man would never fly, the television would never succeed commercially, and the telephone would never be widely used. Unlike such dream killers, I know that the future will be different than the present. And I also realize that if I can spot an economic paradigm shift before it occurs, or shortly thereafter, I'll reap huge financial benefits.

Strategic Opportunities Involve Growth Industries

My research paid off big time. I discovered we're entering one of the greatest economic paradigm shifts in world history. In his book *The Roaring 2000s,* Harry S. Dent Jr. notes that "new technologies, industries, products and services are again about to burst forth. This will mark the real beginning of the information revolution—*but it hasn't really happened yet!*"[13] When I read that last phrase I rocked back in my chair and said, "What does he mean, *yet?*" Dent went on to say, "Sure, a great many businesses have been leveraging the power of the Internet for the last few years, but we won't see the new era of network-based commerce and living until consumers move online in huge numbers, and use the Internet for more than casual information and entertainment."[14]

If I can spot an economic paradigm shift before it occurs, or shortly thereafter, I'll reap huge financial benefits.

I'm convinced we're entering an age in which the Internet will change the way we work, play, buy, and sell (it already is, yet it's only beginning, like a swelling wave). But my study also revealed that the opportunity is much bigger than I ever imagined. And the opportunity to cash in will last until around 2020. I knew the tide was in and I needed to get on board or I'd miss the opportunity altogether.

Strategic Opportunities Catch the Generational Wave

Both Dent Jr., in his book *The Roaring 2000s,* and William Strauss and Neil Howe, in their book *The Fourth Turning,* conclude that every forty years a new generation is formed through birth and immigration. These new generations move through very predictable personal and family spending cycles that peak, on average, at around forty-six to forty-seven years old for the head of the household. This causes boom periods that last twenty-six to twenty-nine years, followed by burst periods after the generation has peaked in its spending that last twelve to fourteen years.

The Internet is to the coming economic boom what the moving assembly line was to the Roaring Twenties.

The Henry Ford generation drove an economic and stock-market boom from 1900 to 1929—the era of Good Feelings to the Roaring Twenties. The Bob Hope generation drove up stocks and our economy from 1942 through 1968. Each of those booms was followed by an economic downturn—first the Great Depression of 1929 and then the off-and-on recessions from 1970 until 1982. Now, the massive Baby Boom generation is driving the greatest economic expansion in history. It started in late 1982, and according to Dent, it will continue until 2008–2009.[15] I'm convinced that his estimate is conservative and that the boom will last until 2020.

The more I investigated what was happening in the world around me, the more I realized the coming decade would provide me with strategic opportunities for significant business and economic growth.

Log on Because the Internet Is the Key

The Internet is to the coming economic boom what the moving assembly line was to the Roaring Twenties. It is the key productivity lever that will rapidly feed new technologies, products, and services into the mainstream economy. It's crucial for you to realize that widespread use of the Internet will fundamentally change the way we handle our business at home and at the office. Whereas the assembly-line shift was a production revolution, this will be a revolution in distribution and marketing.[16]

Knowing what I know now, if I could go back to the early days of the Industrial Revolution, I would jump at the chance to partner with Henry Ford. In a similar vein, those living a hundred years in the future will marvel at the wealth created in the early part of the twenty-first century by those who jumped on the e-commerce train. In a few years every television in the United States will be a portal to the Internet. Instead of fighting traffic and standing in long checkout lines, people will shop at Internet malls.

Instead of fighting traffic and standing in long checkout lines, people will shop at Internet malls.

The more I understood the coming impact of the Internet, the more I realized Faust may have presented me with the strategic opportunity of a lifetime—an opportunity greater than anything Henry Ford could have offered me. But before drawing that conclusion I had to talk with someone who was successful in e-commerce.

PRINCIPLE FOUR
TALK WITH PEOPLE WHO ARE
RIDING THE WAVE

As Lynn and I waited in the family room of our Charleston home, we knew that God had been good to us. Our home, built in 1827, had withstood storms for over 170 years. It had even survived an earthquake that tumbled less stable structures. Like our home, we had survived a few storms of our own, including financial ruin of my trucking business—a loss facilitated by the management team I put in place when I retired at age forty-five. My company, which took over twenty-three years to build and employed two thousand people, had come and gone. Lynn and I had been asking God for an opportunity that I could leverage to make my dream of serving others come true…an opportunity that would enable us to create wealth.

The day we met with Bubba Pratt in our home I wore my custom-made suit and Hermes tie, and Lynn wore a dress. Bubba had on a golf shirt, shorts, and sandals and carried a bottle of water in his right hand. Faust had already told me about the massive wealth Bubba had built. I wasn't interested in the money; I wanted to see what kind of man it took to succeed in an affiliated marketing e-commerce business.

The more we talked, the more my guard came down.

Eventually, I asked Bubba, "Do you think I could succeed at this new business."

He fixed his blue eyes on me and said, "Joe, you can change."

I'd never had anyone speak to me like that. He saw right though the facade of fancy clothes and antique furniture. He saw a broken man who knew how to dream big but needed a new challenge in order to grow as a person.

Before Bubba and I talked I knew e-commerce was the economic wave of the future. After he left I knew he was the kind of man with whom I wanted to trust my family's future. My dream-maker pattern of research indicated that Faust had truly presented me with a strategic opportunity that I needed to pursue.

PRINCIPLE FIVE
IF IT CHECKS OUT—DON'T WAIT, SEIZE THE OPPORTUNITY

Since that meeting with Faust and Bubba over four years ago, I've built an e-commerce business that will allow me to make more money this year than I ever paid myself in salary as the CEO of a $150 million a year trucking company. And the income is residual. But more importantly, I seized an opportunity that promises to help me fulfill my dream of lifting up others and enabling them to find the same success.

Whenever I address audiences around the country, I always conclude by telling them about the day my catcher, Dan Scarper, walked out to the pitching mound and handed me that baseball and said, "Joe, this is the moment you've been waiting for your entire life." I then reach into a ball bag sitting at my feet and pull out baseballs that I hand to the people sitting in the audience. I do this because I want them to leave with a tangible reminder that very soon they will be offered an opportunity they've been preparing for their entire lives. An opportunity they must seize.

If I could reach out to you from this page, I'd drop a ball into your hands right now. But since I can't, imagine that I have. And use that imaginary baseball as a reminder to seize the opportunities that God brings across your path.

Dream Maker Summary

- Know that opportunities occur when the elements needed for their dream to be realized come together at the same time.
- Build the present on the future.
- Stay open to unexpected opportunities.
- Study opportunities to see if they're strategic.
- Talk with people who are riding the wave of success.
- Immediately seize strategic opportunities.

GIVE AWAY LOVE

*Dream makers know that love is the glue
that holds life together.*

Before 1967 Gale Sayers had never had a close relationship with a white man. That all changed when he and Brian Piccolo became running backs for the Chicago Bears and ended up rooming together. Not only was their interracial friendship a first for the two athletes; it was a first in professional football. In fact, Piccolo had never even known a black person.

Their natural affinity for each other grew from a shared sense of humor. Before a 1969 exhibition game in Washington an earnest young reporter entered their hotel room for an interview.

"How do you two get along?" he asked.

At a time when African Americans and Caucasians were

still segregated in parts of the United States, Piccolo gave a tongue-in-cheek answer the reporter didn't expect. "We're okay as long as he doesn't use the bathroom," the running back said with a straight face.

Uncertain how to respond, the reporter asked, "What do you talk about?"

"Mostly race relations," Gale said as he held back his laughter.

"Nothing but the normal racist stuff," Piccolo added.

Growing increasingly uncomfortable but determined to get a story, the reporter asked them who they would most want for a roommate.

"Well, if you mean what white Italian fullback from Wake Forest would I want for a roommate," Sayers said, "I'd have to say Pick."

Of course, the friendship between the men ultimately became a movie, *Brian's Song*. As the movie beautifully depicts, behind the laughter existed a deep bond of love. Indeed, it became one of the most celebrated friendships in professional sports. And then tragedy hit. In 1969 cancer cut down Brian Piccolo. Though he tried to play through the season Piccolo spent more time in the hospital than on the football field. Instead of withdrawing from his dying friend, Gale Sayers left immediately after games and flew across the country to be at his side.

As the season drew to a close they planned, with their wives, to share a table at the Professional Football Writers annual dinner in New York, where Sayers was to be given the George S. Halas Award as the most courageous player in professional football. Weakened by cancer, Pick couldn't make the trip and ended up in his bed at home. At the ceremony, Gale Sayers received the reward, but his heart remained with his friend. The ordinarily stoic black athlete, tears running down his cheeks, had this to say:

> You flatter me by giving me this award, but I tell you here and now that I accept it for Brian Piccolo. Brian Piccolo is the man of courage who should receive the George S. Halas Award. I love Brian Picolo and I'd like you to love him. Tonight, when you hit your knees, please ask God to love him too.[17]

There are no four words in the English language that a person wants to hear more than the words *I love* followed by his or her first and last name. The three most desired words a person can hear are "I love you." Yet, how often do you hear men tell each other that? Indeed, how often do you hear anyone share those three words?

Most people are like the man whose wife of thirty years asked him, "Do you still love me?" He looked at her in surprise, cocked his head to one side, and reflected on the question. The man then nodded his head and said, "If I'm not mistaken, I told you I loved you on the day we got married. And until I tell you differently, what I said then still goes."

Dream makers know that money and the other trappings of success are nothing more than a lubricant for relationships.

Dream makers know that money and the other trappings of success are nothing more than a lubricant for relationships.

Without loving friends and family members, all the money, toys, and power in the world are meaningless.

Nobody illustrates this truth better than the late Howard Hughes. He was the world's ultimate mystery—so secretive, so reclusive, so enigmatic, that for more than fifteen years no one could say for certain that he was alive, much less how he looked or acted.

If anybody seemed to have achieved his dream, it was Howard Hughes. He was one of the world's richest men with the destinies of thousands of people, perhaps even governments, at his disposal, yet he lived a sunless, joyless, half-lunatic life. In his later years he fled from one resort hotel to another—Las Vegas, Nicaragua, Acapulco— and his physical appearance became odder and odder (that's an understatement). His straggly beard hung to his waist, and his hair reached the middle of his back. His fingernails were two inches long, and his toenails hadn't been trimmed for so long they resembled corkscrews.

Dream makers know that love is the glue that holds life together.

Hughes was married for thirteen years to Jean Peters, one of the most beautiful women in the world. But never in that time were the two seen together in public, and there is no record of their ever having been photographed together. Eventually they divorced.

Hughes once said, "Every man has his price or a guy like me couldn't exist." Yet no amount of money could buy him the affection of his associates. Most of his employees who broke their silence after his death reported their disgust for him.

Why was Howard Hughes so isolated and lonely? Why with his almost unlimited wealth, hundreds of aides, and countless beautiful women, was he so entirely alone at his death? Why did no one cry at his funeral?

The answer is simple. Hughes lost sight of the fact that people are to be loved and things are to be used. He loved money, power, and toys, and he used people. He chose to manipulate people rather than love them. Howard Hughes didn't create a dream but a nightmare.[18]

It's crucial for you to grasp the truth that no amount of financial success will give you a fulfilling and happy life. Lesson 6 follows Lesson 5 because as you seize strategic opportunities and begin to build wealth, you'll be tempted to sacrifice relationships. Dream makers know that love is the glue that holds life together. It's the music that brings joy. It's the wind that fills our emotional sails and pushes us forward.

With that reality in mind, I'm going to share with you two dream-maker principles that will enable you give away love.

PRINCIPLE ONE
ACCEPT PEOPLE UNCONDITIONALLY

Everybody, and I mean *everybody*, is a "ten" somewhere. And everybody needs to *feel* that the people he associates with— family, friends, and coworkers—recognize his uniqueness and value him for it. Unfortunately, we live in a world that seldom acknowledges the immeasurable value of an individual. Indeed, most of are accustomed to "winning" the approval of others just as a pitcher must "win" a ball game. We have to look good, smell good, talk good, play good, and hang around with people who achieve the same standards of excellence.

It's a painful fact of life that in addition to being a ten some-where, everyone is also a three somewhere (I picked the number three at random—I could have said zero, because in some areas I'm a zero). A great orator may have weak analytical skills. A talented businessperson may have little patience with children. Michael Jordan may be able to dunk a basketball but would make a poor jockey (can you just imagine him riding a thoroughbred at the Kentucky Derby?). Most of us are aware of our strengths *and* weaknesses. In fact, we spend considerable time highlighting our strengths and hiding our weaknesses. Why? Because we fear that once people see our flaws they'll reject us.

People crave friends who accept them— warts and all.

I'm convinced that people crave friends who accept them—warts and all! They are starved for relationships that are not governed by their ability to maintain a flawless standard of behavior, especially when somebody else has written that standard.

Dream makers understand that fundamental truth. That's why they choose to accept people unconditionally. Now don't misunderstand me. I'm not implying that acceptance means religious or political agreement or the condoning of a particular lifestyle. Instead, I mean that regardless of what somebody believes or how they live, I have chosen to accept them just as they are—no strings attached.

Such unconditional acceptance is nurtured by a willingness to focus on the best in others, not the worst. Several years ago the *Wall Street Journal* dedicated an entire page to declaring the importance of each individual. Here's what the page said:

How Important Are You?
    More than
    You think.
    A rooster
    Minus a hen
    Equals
    No baby chicks.

    Kellogg minus
    A farmer
    Equals
    No corn flakes.

    If the nail
    Factory closes
    What good is the
    hammer factory?

    Pederewski's
    Genius wouldn't have
    Amounted to much
    If the
    Piano tuner
    Hadn't shown up.

    A cracker maker
    Will do better
    If there's a
    Cheesmaker.

    The most skillful
    Surgeon needs

The ambulance driver
Who delivers the
Patient.

Just as Rogers
Needed Hammerstein
You need someone
And someone
Needs you.

Dream makers realize that everyone is a ten somewhere, and they diligently seek to find out where. Once they do, they focus on that trait, celebrate it, and communicate unconditional acceptance.

"Okay," you may be saying, "that sounds good, but how do you do it?"

Actually, the answer is simple. I do two things. First, when I meet someone or am developing a friendship with someone, I ask questions. I probe. I urge the person to talk about who he is and what he likes to do. When I hear a note of enthusiasm in his voice, I know he's talking about something important to him. I know I'm getting close to his heart, his passion, and his main interest.

Dream makers realize that everyone is a ten somewhere, and they diligently seek to find out where.

Secondly, when I see someone drawing a circle that leaves me out, I draw a bigger one that brings him in. I continually reach out to the person and let him know he's important to me—regardless of whatever differences may exist between us.

One afternoon I called my friend Jimmy Gallant and asked what he was doing. "Come over and see," he said.

I hopped into my Range Rover and headed for the inner city. Jimmy's an African American who serves as the chaplain for the Charleston police department and heads up a ministry to inner-city kids, gang members, and poor families. He cares for the neglected and forgotten segment of our city.

A few minutes later we were together, and he offered to show me what he had done with some money I had given him a few days earlier. He hopped in my car, and ten minutes later we pulled up in front of a housing project and went upstairs to a dilapidated apartment. A young mother and a brood of children greeted us at the front door.

Several days earlier Jimmy had used the money I sent him to buy groceries for this mother and her children. There had been nothing to eat in their house for days. Jimmy looked at me and said, "Brother, this is what I did with your money."

I looked down and saw a snotty-nosed, dirty-haired, filth-covered two-year-old boy staring up at me with big brown eyes and outstretched arms.

"Pick him up," Jimmy said. I was thinking, *Not me. You're not talking to me.*

After a moment's hesitation I squatted down, grabbed the child under the shoulders, and held him against my chest—and my expensive suit. In that moment I no longer saw a boy in need of a bath and clean clothes. I saw a child in need of love. And I understood, for the first time, why Jimmy Gallant turned down an offer from one of Detroit's big car manufacturers to own a car dealership. He knew, as all dream makers know, that everyone needs unconditional love. And he has devoted his life to extending the love of Jesus to forgotten people. From him I discovered the importance of drawing circles of love that include people unlike me. Doing that means I need to understand how people are different from me and communicate love in a way that works for them.

PRINCIPLE TWO
MASTER THE LANGUAGES OF LOVE

In his excellent book *The Five Languages of Love,* Gary Chapman draws a parallel between spoken languages and what he calls "love languages."[19] In the area of linguistics, there are major language groups: Japanese, Chinese, Spanish, English, Portuguese, Greek, German, and French to name a few. Most of us grew up learning the language of our parents and siblings, and it became our native tongue. Later, we may have applied significant effort to learn an additional language. This becomes our secondary language. If we speak only our primary language and encounter someone who speaks only his or her primary language, which is different from ours, we may experience a communication breakdown.

Chapman suggests that in the area of love, we all have a primary emotional love language (For a more in depth look at the five love languages, read Chapman's book—it's a keeper!). The problem is that we often assume everyone else speaks our love language, so we express affection for him or her in the way we want it expressed to us. If he or she speaks a different love language, our efforts are as effective as they would be if we tried to speak English to someone who only understands German.[20]

That's why it's so important to know the five love languages and go out of your way to communicate affection in the language of the person you're interacting with.

Love Language #1: Words of Affirmation

Because this is my primary love language, it's easy for me to verbally affirm others. I not only make it a habit to look for the good in others; I tell them what I see. And I do it in a straight-forward way.

"You're look absolutely glamorous," I tell my wife, Lynn, when she's decked out in a black dinner dress.

"I saw your show this morning," I tell Meredith, my middle daughter, who anchors the local NBC morning news. "You did a super job covering that breaking story."

"I'm privileged to be on your team," I tell Dr. James Yanney, one of my business partners.

I praise people for their diligence, faithfulness, selflessness, generosity, empathy, vision, patience, kindness, joyfulness, gentleness, self-control, faith, and every other positive trait I see in their character or behavior.

Of course, I hadn't been married long before I realized that Lynn's primary love language wasn't the same as mine.

Love Language #2: Quality Time

I know Lynn relishes the affirmation I give her. But if she had to choose between a timely compliment and a walk along the riverfront by our house, she'd choose a walk any day. Why? Because quality time is her primary love language. I can compliment her all day, and it won't have nearly the effect thirty minutes of focused time will have.

Words of affirmation focus on what's being said, whereas quality time focuses on what's being heard. When I affirm someone, I'm talking. When I spend quality time with her, I drawing her out with questions. I'm focused on her.

I praise people for their diligence, faithfulness, selflessness, generosity, empathy, vision, patience, kindness, joyfulness, gentleness, self-control, faith, and every other positive trait I see in their character or behavior.

Those whose primary love language is quality time don't feel they've engaged in quality time when they sit beside someone and watch a television show or movie. Nor do they consider it quality time if the person they're with reads the paper, talks on the phone, or engages in another activity while they're talking.

My friend Bill Perkins told me that his wife's primary love language is quality time. In order to tell her he loves her, he agreed to a weekly date night during which they took ballroom dancing lessons. He boasted that he not only learned how to do the West Coast Swing and Hustle, but he also strengthened his marriage at the same time.

Of course, for some people neither words of affirmation nor quality time is used to express love. These individuals may prefer the third love language.

Love Language #3: Receiving Gifts

All of us have childhood memories that center around those times of the year when we received gifts. Every Christmas my parents would deck out a Christmas tree with lights, tinsel, ornaments, and a star on the top. As December 25 approached they would begin piling presents under the tree. On Christmas Eve I could hardly sleep—in fact I usually didn't—because I was so excited about the presents waiting under tree. I suspect you've had similar experiences.

Birthdays are the second time during the year when we traditionally receive gifts. If I hadn't gotten gifts at Christmas, or on my birthday, I would have been hurt. Why? Because gifts are tangible symbols of love. When a man or woman looks at his or her wedding ring, he or she is reminded of the love of his or her marriage partner.

Chances are you either enjoy giving gifts, or you know someone who does. Maybe gifts aren't that big a deal to you, and you find it hard to remember to give them to other people. If that's true, then it's time for you to make up your mind that you'll give gifts whether or not you think it's important. After all, many people won't know you love them unless you give gifts.

The most valuable gift you can give is your presence at a friend's side during a time of crisis.

You could be thinking, *But I don't have money for gifts.* Money isn't important. Some of the most meaningful gifts I've ever received were those made by my children at school or church. Occasionally, the most valuable gift you can give is your presence at a friend's side during a time of crisis.

If you want to show love, be sure and practice generosity with gifts.

Love Language # 4: Acts of Service

You'll encounter many people, and you may be one of them, who believe words of affirmation, quality time, and timely gifts are an *easy* way of saying, "I love you." For them the most genuine expression of love comes in the form of service.

Ted "the Bear" Nanney is a business partner of mine who is the ultimate servant. He constantly searches out ways he can help other people. At business meetings he'll show up early and make sure the chairs are set up and the other arrangements are in order. My tendency is to *tell* Ted how much I appreciate him. What I've learned is that he doesn't need much verbal affirmation. He shows love by serving, and if I want to communicate love to him, I have to do it with acts of service.

I've found that standing beside him and helping out with an aspect of his work—working alongside him—communicates more affection than a page of verbal affirmation. I also enjoy serving others. In our e-commerce business, the bigger the servant, the bigger the business grows.

Every time I think of communicating love through service, I think of the night Jesus washed the disciples' feet. While his team of disciples argued about who would be the greatest in His kingdom, Jesus wrapped a towel around His waist, took a pitcher of water and a basin, and cleaned twenty-four dirty feet—including Judas's. What an act of love!

Love Language # 5: Physical Touch

Several years ago researchers discovered the profound power of human touch. A team of researchers tracked the recovery rate of patients whose doctors frequently placed a hand on their shoulder or forearm in comparison to patients whose doctors never touched them. Amazingly, patients whose doctors touched them recovered from illness or surgery much faster than those who were not touched.

The researchers speculated that the touch of the doctor released endorphins (the body's natural opiatelike substance that alleviates pain and discomfort while elevating the mood) that actually facilitate healing. Similar studies of young children demonstrate that children who are frequently hugged or touched in other affirming ways experience better physical and emotional health.

Patients whose doctors touched them recovered from illness or surgery much faster than those who were not touched.

In a world that is increasingly alert to inappropriate touching (and rightly so), it's crucial that all touching be appropriate for the situation. A hand on the shoulder or a pat on the back can tell a friend I'm there to support him. For someone whose primary love language is touch, such an act communicates deep affection.

I recently gave a bear hug to a friend and then told him, "I love you." He became teary-eyed and said, "I've never had a man hug me before."

"Well, you have now," I said.

Something about that encounter pierced a protective wall he had spent a lifetime erecting. If you're a hands-off kind of person, you might consider coming out of your comfort zone and reaching out. Try placing a hand on a friend's shoulder or giving a pat on the back. You may discover that it's the only way some people will know you care for them. Why? Because touch is their primary love language.

A BROTHER LIKE THAT

A story is told about a man named Paul who received an automobile from his brother for Christmas. As Paul left his office on Christmas Eve, he saw a street urchin standing on the edge of the curb admiring his car. "Is this your car, Mister?" he asked.

As Paul slipped the key into the door lock, he nodded his head and smiled. "My brother gave it to me for Christmas."

"You mean your brother gave it to you, and it didn't cost you nothin'?" the boy asked. The boy shook his head from side to side and said, "Boy, I wish…" Then he hesitated.

Instinctively, Paul knew that the boy was about to wish for a brother who would give him a car. Instead, he said something that jarred Paul to his heels.

"I wish," the boy went on, "*I* could be a brother like that."

Paul gazed at the boy in astonishment and then asked if he would like to go for a ride in the new car.

"I'd love that," he replied, without a moment's hesitation.

After a short ride, the boy turned, and with his eyes aglow, said, "Mister, would you drive in front of my house?"

Paul smiled as he followed the boy's instructions and headed for his home. He sensed that the boy wanted to show his neighbors that he could ride home in a fancy, new automobile. Once more, Paul was wrong in his judgment. "Will you stop where those two steps are?" the boy asked.

After Paul stopped the car and put it in park, the boy jumped out and ran up the steps. A few moments later he came out of the house carrying his disabled brother in his arms. He sat him down on the bottom step, then squeezed up against him and pointed to the car.

"There she is, Buddy, just like I told you upstairs. His brother gave it to him for Christmas, and it didn't cost him a cent. And some day I'm gonna' give you one just like it…then you can see for yourself all the pretty things in the Christmas windows that I've been telling you about."

Paul climbed out of the car and lifted the child into the front seat of his car. The shining-eyed brother climbed in beside him, and the three of them began a memorable holiday ride.

That child understood something every dream maker must learn. He knew the truth of Jesus' words, "It is more blessed to give than receive."[21]

DREAM MAKER SUMMARIES

- Know the value of love and give it away.
- Accept people unconditionally.
- Know that everybody is a ten somewhere and diligently seek to find out where.
- Master the five love languages.
- Give words of affirmation to those who need them.
- Spend quality time with those who need it.
- Offer gifts to those who need them.
- Serve those who need to be served.
- Offer a pat on the back or hug to those who need it.
- Know that it's more blessed to give than receive.

PERSEVERANCE LEADS TO SUCCESS

Dream makers know that their vision of the future will only become reality through peristence.

There is a dream-maker principle for life that says: *Perseverance leads to success.* Once you grasp the reliability of this principle, it will transform the way you view hardship. No longer will you view adversity as a threat to your dream, but as an unavoidable step in the process of building it.

All of us want success without hardship. We want the body of a weight lifter and the endurance of a marathon runner. But we want them without paying the price of hard work. The truth is that adversity is to the dream maker's life what the weight room is to a professional football player or the road is to a world-class runner.

The difference between dreamers and dream makers is

that dream makers expect adversity. They know it will hit hard, like a body blow in a championship fight, and they've prepared themselves to absorb the blow and move on.

Every setback, disappointment, obstacle, and hardship will strengthen you as a person and improve your methods of operation, if you let it.

Nobody who has seen the realization of his dream did so without overcoming numerous obstacles and setbacks. Every setback, disappointment, obstacle, and hardship will strengthen you as a person and improve your methods of operation *if you let it*. The form your dream takes in its realization may be different than what you originally imagined. It may happen at a time other than what you originally planned. But if you persevere, you will succeed. Remember, *even the snail made it into the ark*. In fact, I'm convinced that the only way you will fail is if you give up.

Dream makers aren't successful because of their personality, education, training, or financial resources. They succeed because they persevere, and they persevere because they've learned the power of a single word: FOCUS. Dream makers refuse to allow anything to divert their attention away from the dream they're pursuing. I realize that in the course of building your dream, you will face hardships along the way. In order to overcome them—which you must do to succeed—it's essential for you to stay focused. In order to help you do that, I'm going to share with you four principles of perseverance. It's crucial for you to read them, study them, and practice them diligently.

PERSEVERANCE PRINCIPLE ONE
FOCUS ON THE DREAM, NOT THE DIVERSION

Several years ago an experiment was conducted in which a team of researchers placed a dozen laboratory mice in a vat of water. As the mice swam in small circles, the researchers would periodically lift out of the water several mice that had been identified with marks on their heads. As the researchers expected, the mice that were lifted out of the water swam far longer than those that weren't. Why? The researchers concluded that those mice hoped that if they swam just a little longer, they would be delivered.

Although I'm no mouse psychologist, I do understand human nature. And I know that in one way all of us are like those mice. Everyone is motivated by hope. As long as we expect a better future, we'll keep swimming, even when our muscles ache and our arms are exhausted.

On those occasions when you feel that you have no more chance of getting out of your mess than those mice had of climbing out of that vat of water, focus on your dream. Rivet your mental attention on what you want tomorrow to bring, not the water (or whatever circumstance is trying to divert your attention). The hope that your dream will someday come true will infuse you with the emotional and physical strength you need to carry on for one more day, week, month, or year. But you must stay focused on your dream!

The hope that your dream will someday come true will infuse you with the emotional and physical strength you need to carry on for one more day, week, month, or year.

Golf immortal Arnold Palmer once learned a painful lesson about the importance of focus. During the final hole of the 1961 Masters Tournament, Palmer had a one-stroke lead and had just hit a rocket of a tee shot far down the middle of the fairway. When the ball rolled to a stop, he smiled, confident that he would sustain his lead.

A few minutes later, as he approached the ball, he saw an old friend standing at the edge of the gallery. He motioned Palmer over, stuck out his hand, and said, "Congratulations!" Palmer took his hand, and as he did, he knew he had lost his focus.

Shaking his head, Palmer returned to the ball, took a few practice swings, and then lofted the ball into the middle of a sand trap. On the following shot he smacked the ball out of the sand and over the far edge of the green.

Later Palmer told a reporter, "You don't forget a mistake like that. You just learn from it and become determined that you will never do it again."

As you pursue your dream don't make the mistake of allowing distractions to divert your attention away from your destination. Focus on your dream not the distractions.

PERSEVERANCE PRINCIPLE TWO
FOCUS ON SOLUTIONS, NOT SETBACKS

Every setback you'll ever face is nothing more than an opportunity to figure out a better way to pursue your dream. On the day I realized my trucking company faced a financial crisis that would require a pile of money and years of effort to correct, I knew my dream of serving others could be derailed.

During those dark days I could identify with the story about the Lone Ranger and Tonto, his Native American sidekick. As the two friends rode across the prairie one afternoon, a band of a thousand hostile Apaches appeared to the north. The two horsemen turned to the south, where another thousand Apaches were attacking. As they spun around they saw a thousand Apaches wearing war paint racing toward them from the east and west.

Every setback you'll ever face is nothing more than an opportunity to figure out a better way to pursue your dream.

"Well, it looks like it's curtains for us," the Lone Ranger said.

Tonto turned to the masked man and said, "What you mean, '*us*,' Paleface?"

As my trucking business teetered on the brink of failure, I felt abandoned by my bankers and deserted by my friends. I felt as alone and vulnerable as the Lone Ranger did. But as a dream maker I knew that hidden in the setback were a host of solutions. I just needed to find them.

Without going into the details, I'll tell you that I devised a plan to salvage the company. But I did something even more important. Through the setback, I discovered that I wanted to build a business where I could spend more time with my family and create the kind of residual wealth that would provide me with a platform for helping others. Had that setback not occurred I would never have been open to the e-commerce business that has brought my dream into reality.

Dream makers refuse to fixate on setbacks. I love the story of Thomas Edison, who performed over ten thousand unsuccessful experiments in an effort to find a filament for incandescent light-bulbs. Now remember that Edison not only had to cope with the repeated failures, but also with people who criticized his ideas and methods.

When he arrived home and announced to his wife that the ten thousandth experiment had failed she asked, "Aren't you discouraged?"

"Discouraged? How could I be discouraged? I now know ten thousand things that don't work." Thomas Edison made his dream come true because he focused on solutions, not setbacks.

Remember, for every setback there are several solutions. Focus on finding the solutions, not crying over the setbacks.

Remember, for every setback there are several solutions. Focus on finding the solutions, not crying over the setbacks.

PERSEVERANCE PRINCIPLE THREE
FOCUS ON THE POTENTIAL, NOT THE PROBLEM

When I decided to pursue my e-commerce business, numerous business friends told me I was crazy. I explained that the e-mall would enable the public to buy anything they needed and have it delivered to their doorstep.

"It will never work," they insisted.

I told them that the savings in time and money would attract people like a candy store attracts kids.

"People would rather shop at walk-in malls," they noted.

"It will take too long to generate income," they said.

"You're a trucking executive," someone reminded me. "Stick with what you know."

"People don't *really* make money in *that* kind of business," they argued.

If I weren't a dream maker I would have listened to those well-intentioned people. Instead, I did what every dream maker does—I focused on the potential, not the problem. And by focusing on my dream I joined the ranks of other dream makers

Arnold Schwarzenegger's family begged him to get a "respectable" job. They repeatedly asked him, "How long will you go on training in a gymnasium and living in a dream world?" Schwarzenegger focused on his dream of becoming Mr. Universe, and one day his hard work paid off.

Weeks before she launched her successful business, Mary Kay Ash's attorney urged her to focus on the problems she would face, not the dream she would build. He told her to "Liquidate the business right now and recoup whatever cash you can. If you don't, you'll end up penniless."

When we focus on our problems instead of our dream, precious energy and enthusiasm are drained away.

Ray Charles's teacher once told him, "You can't play the piano, and God knows you can't sing. You'd better learn how to weave chairs so you can support yourself." Problems. Problems. Problems. Some people choose to see only problems. Notice that I said they *choose* to see problems. When we focus on our problems instead of our dreams, precious energy and enthusiasm are drained away.

None of the people I just mentioned chose to focus on the problems they encountered. Instead, they glanced at the problems and focused on their dream. Of course, problems have to be acknowledged, addressed, and overcome. But dream makers refuse to let them be the object of their focus.

PERSEVERANCE PRINCIPLE FOUR
FOCUS ON YOUR FAITH, NOT YOUR FAILURES

One day somebody told me, "I think I've missed Plan A for my life."

"Really?" I said. "What does that mean?"

"It means I've missed God's best."

I occasionally hear this from people who find it easier to blame God for their circumstances than to take responsibility themselves. They believe that they forfeited their future with a past mistake. And they conclude that since God has decided *not* to expand their horizon, it would be useless for them to dream big. "Why fight God?" they ask.

My response usually surprises them. "Well, I'm glad there are twenty-six letters in the alphabet, aren't you?"

"What do you mean?" they ask.

"I mean if you missed Plan A, then it's time you got started on Plan B, or C, or D, or E." I then like to remind them that some of the greatest men and women in the Bible recovered from serious mistakes. For instance:

- Moses committed murder and forty years later led the Israelites out of slavery.
- Samson committed adultery, lost his eyesight and freedom, and then defeated his enemies.
- Sarah laughed at God and then gave birth to Isaac in her

old age and became the mother of a nation (she was ninety and Abraham was one hundred).

- Rahab was a prostitute whose life was filled with mistakes until the day she helped Joshua and the Israelites defeat the fortified city of Jericho.
- Peter denied three times that he knew Jesus and later became a pillar of the early church.

The names of men and women from the Bible and history who recovered from mistakes could fill volumes of books. *The past does not equal the future, and there is no future in the past.* No matter what mistakes you've made in the past God is there to help you succeed in the future. Your responsibility is to tap into His power.

The next time you think your past failures will limit your future successes remember this equation: God + Me = Victory. The truth is that your faith in God will enable you to overcome past failures and future challenges.

No matter what mistakes you've made in the past God is there to help you succeed in the future.

One of my favorite prayers, and one that I pray daily, was given to me by my business partner, Joel Christy. The prayer is found in the Old Testament book of 1 Chronicles 4:9–10, where a long list of men from the tribe of Judah is highlighted. In the middle of that list of names we find the prayer of a man who was more honorable than his brothers. The words of his prayer are profound. "'Oh, that you would bless me and enlarge my territory! Let your hand be with me, and keep me from harm so that I will be free from pain.' And God granted his request."[22]

Jabez realized that the boundary of his success would ultimately be drawn by God, not him. He received God's blessing because he placed his faith in God.

A story is told about a little boy who worked feverishly beside his father in the yard. As the two moved rocks to make a path, the boy struggled in vain to dislodge a boulder from the ground.

If God has given you a dream, then He'll also give you the resources needed to bring it into reality.

"I can't move it," he said between gritted teeth.

"That's because you're not using all of your strength," his dad said.

"Yes, I am," the boy insisted, grunting and straining to move the boulder.

"No, you're not," his dad insisted. "You haven't asked me to help."

The boy stood up, smiled, and said, "Will you help me?" A moment later the two easily rolled the boulder aside.

Like that boy, you need to ask God for his help. And the next time you're tempted to think your past failures will limit your future success, remember: God + Me = Victory.

If God has given you a dream, then He'll also give you the resources needed to bring it into reality. To give you a different perspective on your situation, consider this. According to Einstein's Theory of Relativity, if one ounce of mass were converted into energy, it would produce the amount of energy generated by burning 18 million gallons of gasoline. That would be enough power to enable you to drive your car 360,000,000 miles (14 million trips around the world) if you averaged 20 miles per gallon of gasoline.

That's the amount of energy generated by converting *one* ounce of mass into energy. Yet the sun converts 4,600,000 tons of mass into energy every second. Now consider that our sun is only an average-sized star in the Milky Way Galaxy and the Milky Way consists of over 300 million stars.

And our galaxy is only *one* in a universe of billions of galaxies. It's been estimated that the universe is a great sphere 25 billion light-years across. That means light traveling at the rate of 5,880 trillion miles a year would take 25 billion years to travel from one corner of the universe to another.

In other words, we live in a very big universe that generates an immeasurable amount of power every second. Yet we read in Psalm 104:2 that God stretched out the heavens like a tent. Whenever I consider the size of my failures or problems and compare it to God, I pause and ask myself, "So, what's my problem?"

Occasionally, someone will tell me, "But I don't like to bother God with my problems. They're so small."

Hey, compared to God everything's small. But He's interested in our problems and wants to release *God + Me = Victory* His infinite power on our behalf. But we need to trust Him to do that. Once more, the next time you seem overwhelmed with a failure or problem, remember: God + Me = Victory. That doesn't mean the victory will be immediate or that it will take the form you anticipated. But it does mean ultimate victory will be yours.

SEE THROUGH THE FOG

A thick fog shrouded the coastline of Catalina Island on the morning of July 4, 1952. Later that night fireworks would decorate skies across the United States. But before the festive celebrations, Florence Chadwick would attempt something never done by a woman. Her dream was to swim from Catalina Island to the California coast.

As Florence waded into the salty water the fog prevented her from seeing clearly the boats that accompanied her. Millions watched on television as sharks circled so closely that an attack seemed imminent.

Determined to reach the shore of California, she struggled against cold water, a fear of sharks, strong currents, and physical exhaustion. Less than a mile from the realization of her dream she asked to be pulled from the water. Later, when a reporter asked her why she had given up when the coast loomed so close, she blamed the fog. It obstructed her view. It blinded her reason, her eyes, and her heart. She said, "I'm not excusing myself. But if I could have seen land, I might have made it."

I understand how she felt. I've never attempted to swim the English Channel as Chadwick did in both directions. Nor have I tried to swim from Catalina Island to the California coast (frankly, a twenty-six-mile walk would be plenty of exercise for me). But I have suffered from diversions, setbacks, problems, and past failures that have tempted me to give up.

Fortunately, there's more to the Florence Chadwick's saga. Or, as Paul Harvey says, "Now for the rest of the story."

On a foggy day in September 1952, Florence again waded

into the frigid waters off the coast of Catalina Island. Everything looked the same as it had two months earlier. The fog, sharks, and cold water all threatened her resolve. But this time Florence not only completed the swim; she broke the men's record by two hours. When asked what had changed she told reporters that the only difference was her focus. She focused her mind on an image of the coast and refused to allow anything to divert her attention until she stepped onto the sandy beach.

Like Florence Chadwick, and other dream makers, you must believe that *perseverance leads to success.* And you must focus on your dream because *focus is the key to perseverance.*

DREAM MAKER SUMMARIES

- Know that perseverance leads to success.
- Know that focus is the key to perseverance.
- Focus on their dream, not diversions.
- Focus on solutions, not setbacks.
- Focus on potential, not problems.
- Focus on their faith, not their failures.
- Repeatedly tell themselves: **God + Me = Victory**

MASTER THE ART
OF MENTORING

*Dream makers learn from the success of others
and then pass the lessons along.*

Our home in Charleston is located on a peninsula. It's not uncommon on a windy spring day to see children standing on the bank of the Ashley River flying kites. On those occasions I'm reminded of the times I've held a kite string and felt the wind trying to pull it from my grip. Of course, if I had released the string, the kite would have plummeted into the river. A kite does the flying, but it needs the help of a man, woman, or child to help it take advantage of the wind. Kites don't fly on their own—they must have someone help them.

Like a kite, dream makers can't soar by themselves. They need others to help them get airborne. And they need others to help them stay there. In a word, they need mentors. But the necessity of having mentors isn't the whole story. Dream makers learn from their mentors *so they can mentor others.* They have been lifted to success *so they can elevate others.*

Over the years I've identified five commitments that every mentor makes. While they undoubtedly make additional ones, dream makers work hard at making and keeping these five. Because they're so crucial, we'll look at each one. But first, I want to be sure we share a common understanding of exactly what a mentor is.

WHAT IS A MENTOR?

If you look up the word *mentor* in a dictionary you'll find that the word refers to "a wise and trusted counselor or teacher." The original person named Mentor is a figure in the *Odyssey,* an epic poem by the Greek poet Homer. Mentor is the male guardian and tutor of Telemachus, the son of the poem's central character, Odysseus. While Odysseus is away fighting at Troy and then finding his way home, Mentor raises Telemachus into manhood. In the character of Mentor we find a trusted guide committed to training the next generation. That's the essence of what it means to be a mentor.

When the student is ready, the teacher will appear.

Mentors are trusted men and women who devote themselves to training somebody less experienced or knowledgeable. Mentors are player-coaches who not only explain how something is done; they demonstrate how it's done. I'm convinced that when the student is ready, the teacher will appear.

Because dreaming is easier than doing, dream makers

know that it's crucial for them to get directions from someone who has already traveled the road to success. As they see their dream take shape, they know it's equally important for them to look for others to whom they can show the way.

THE FIVE COMMITMENTS OF A MENTOR

Over the course of my life the three men who mentored me were my father, Bobby Richardson, and Bubba Pratt. Each of those men left a life changing impression on me. And nothing each man did was more important than the first commitment of mentoring.

Commitment #1: "I believe in you!"

My dad was physically exhausted when he came home from work every day. I have no doubt that he would have enjoyed relaxing in a recliner and watching television. Instead, he grabbed a catcher's mitt and a baseball and played catch with me. My dad believed that, with a lot of work, I could become a great pitcher. And his faith fueled my desire to excel.

Later, when I attended the University of South Carolina, I had the privilege of playing for the great Bobby Richardson. During my junior year I tore the rotator cuff in my right shoulder—ending my pitching career before I had played in the big league. It would have been understandable if Bobby had cut me from the team or just let me ride the bench. Instead, during my senior year he made me a catcher. Why?

Because mentors see our potential, they believe in us and help us believe in ourselves.

117

Because he believed I could still make an important contribution to the team. His belief in me was supported by my teammates, who elected me team captain.

Years later, when I decided to leave the trucking business, another mentor entered my life. I'll never forget the day Bubba Pratt promised to do everything he could to help me succeed in the e-commerce business. Time and again he communicated his belief in me. And time and again his confidence in my future success acted like a turbocharger thrusting me forward. Bubba didn't just tell me I could win the game of e-commerce; he showed me how to do it.

It's easy for a person to lose touch with his dream...to forget his high calling...to ignore his passion. Because mentors see our potential, they believe in us and help us believe in ourselves.

We all face the danger of becoming like the baby tiger that got lost in a herd of goats. After hanging around with the goats for a while, the cub started viewing himself as a goat. He nibbled green grass like the rest of the herd. He nursed the mother goat like the rest of the kids. He even made bleating noises just like a goat.

One day a tiger came roaring through the herd of goats, scattering them like bowling pins. After all the goats had disappeared into the trees, the tiny tiger continued munching on grass as though nothing unusual had happened.

The big tiger approached the cub and roared so loudly the ground shook. The cub looked up and bleated softly in reply. Shocked, the adult tiger roared again. Once more he heard a soft bleat.

The tiger thought to himself, *This is horrible!* He used his powerful jaw and grabbed the baby tiger by the nape of his neck and carried him over to a clear pool of water. There he suspended the little tiger over the water so he could see his reflection. When the cub looked down, to his amazement, he saw a tiger, not a goat, staring back at him.

After the big tiger put him down, the baby once again bleated. Determined to break the spell the goats had placed on the young tiger, the adult cuffed him upside the head every time he bleated. Before long the cub sounded more like a tiger than a goat.

Likewise, every time the baby tiger bent down to eat grass, the adult would push him over. Soon, the grown tiger introduced the cub to the taste of warm meat. In a short time the cub began to act like a tiger. Why? Because when he met a tiger who saw his potential and confronted him with that which he was created to be, it brought out of him what he was intended to be.

That's what my mentors have done for me, and that's what I'm committed to do for others. But there's a second commitment mentors make that's as crucial as the first.

Commitment #2: "I'm dedicated to you."

You've probably never heard of Charlie Beacham—a southern gentleman who worked for the Ford Motor Company as its eastern regional manager in Chester, Pennsylvania. And you're probably not familiar with the name Lido—the young salesman he mentored.

The son of poor Italian immigrant parents, Lido had been

hired to work in fleet sales at the Chester office. One day Beacham noticed Lido walking across the garage with his head down.

"Hey, Lido," he said, throwing an arm around the young man's shoulders, "what are you so down about?"

"Mr. Beacham," the salesman replied, "you've got thirteen salesmen selling in thirteen zones, and you're looking at the guy who finished number thirteen in sales this month."

"C'mon, kid!" Beacham barked. "Don't let that get you down! Somebody's gotta be last!" He slapped the young man on the back and walked toward his car. As he opened the driver's door, he turned and called out to Lido, "But listen! Just don't be last two months in a row, hear?"

As a mentor, Charlie Beacham was dedicated to the young salesman. He gave Lido advice, showed him the ropes of the business, and instructed him in the kind of character needed for success in business and in life.

"Always remember," Beacham once told him, "that everyone makes mistakes. Trouble is, most people won't own up to their mistakes. Some guys blame them on the weather, their wives, their kids, their dogs—but never on themselves. If you foul up around here, I want you to come to me and own up to it, no excuses, no alibis."

Charlie Beacham gradually increased Lido's responsibilities. As Lido sharpened his skills as a salesman, Beacham had him teach local dealers how to increase truck sales. He made him responsible for the development of a handbook for the company. He even sent Lido on sales and training trips up and down the eastern seaboard.

Lido didn't just learn about the car business from Charlie Beacham; he learned how his mentor's dedication to his success could transform him from a last-place car salesman to a leader. Charlie Beacham, Lido later recalled, had "more impact on my life than any person other than my father…. He was a great motivator—the kind of guy you'd charge up the hill for, even though you knew very well you could get killed in the process…. He was not only my mentor; he was more than that. He was my *tormentor*. But I love him!"

Lido took the knowledge, skills, character, and maturity he acquired under the mentorship of Charlie Beacham and put it to good use throughout his career at Ford and at the Chrysler Corporation.

The ultimate test of his skill and character came in the early 1980s when, as Chrysler's chief executive officer, he led the company from the brink of disaster ($4.75 billion in debt in 1980) to stratospheric heights of success ($925 million in the black in 1983). Today, as you've already guessed, Lido is better known as Lee Iacocca. Auto industry analysts attribute the amazing turnaround of the Chrysler Corporation to this one man. Iacocca, in turn, gives much of the credit for the shaping of his own leadership skills to his mentor, Charlie Beacham.[23]

Mentors dedicate themselves to the development of the person they're training.

Like Charlie Beacham, mentors dedicate themselves to the development of the person they're training.

They dedicate their time—like my dad when he played catch with me day after day, month after month, and year after year.

They dedicate their insight—like Bobby Richardson when he transitioned me from a pitcher to a catcher.

They dedicate their emotional energy—like Bubba when he encouraged me in the development of my e-commerce business.

Mentors dedicate themselves to the individuals they're developing. And one way they express their dedication is by making the third commitment.

Commitment #3: "I'll always encourage you."

Regardless of what path your life takes it will be littered with obstacles. You will face hardship, heartache, disappointment, and even despair. There are no detours around the obstacles or shortcuts through them. Because of this painful fact of life, dream makers must have *someone* whose words will give them a lift when times are tough. They must have a mentor who will encourage them to keep on keeping on when they feel like giving up.

Joyce Landorf's book *Balcony People* is among my favorites because she so clearly explains the importance of affirmation. Her own understanding was facilitated by the words of author and speaker Keith Miller. In her book Joyce says she was *"blown away"* when she heard Keith urge his audience to envision their minds as though they were housed in a clear glass sphere or circle. The bottom two-thirds of the globe is filled with the dark, murky water of our unconscious minds. The top third is filled with the pure, clear oxygen of our conscious mind.

Keith then spoke about the people who live in the dark waters of our unconscious mind. They are family or friends, living or dead, who reach up through that black water and grab us. Miller said that Freudian psychologists call these people "basement people."

These are the people who told me, "You'll never be a professional baseball player." "You'll never succeed in the trucking business." "You should give up on your e-commerce business—it will never work."

As you read these words I'm sure you can hear the haunting voices rising from the basement of your mind. They may come from your mother, father, teacher, coach, classmate, friend, boss, or acquaintance. Perhaps they called you "stupid," "lazy," "ugly," or "a failure." And even though the words may have been spoken years ago, they still trouble you.

Fortunately, as Miller pointed out to Landorf, we have the wonderful advantage of "balcony people," who live in the top third of our minds.[24] These are the people who have cheered us on as we run the race of life. I can still hear the words of my father, "One of these days, son, you're going to play in the big leagues." I remember Bobby Richardson telling me, "Hey, Joe, you're the captain of the team. The rotator cuff may keep you from pitching, but it won't keep you from playing." Bubba's words from the balcony echo off the walls of my mind, "Of course you can do it, Joe. You can change."

When times are tough, I remember the words of Jesus, "Peace I give you, my peace I give to you. Not as the world gives, I give unto you." When I felt like giving up, I recalled the words of James, the half-brother of Jesus, "Consider it pure joy when you encounter all kinds of trials because you can know that the testing of your faith produces endurance."

∽

Every mentor I've ever had lived in the balcony of my mind, where he leaned over the railing and cheered me on.

Every mentor I've ever had lived in the balcony of my mind, where he leaned over the railing and cheered me on. And I've made a commitment to those I mentor to live in the balcony of their minds.

I do that by focusing on the positive rather than the negative. Anybody can see someone's weaknesses and point them out. Dream makers *choose* to concentrate on the positive.

I not only focus on the positive; I expect the best from those I'm mentoring. One way I do this is by making the next commitment.

Commitment # 4: "I'll hold you accountable."

C. S. Lewis wrote that lovers, facing each other, don't see the world but only each other. Friends, he said, stand together, facing the world and all it throws at them, shoulder to shoulder. If you substituted the word *mentor* for friend you'd capture the essence of what it means to be accountable to a mentor. Accountability enables a dream maker to set lofty goals with the confidence they'll be reached, because a mentor will be standing at his or her side whenever he's needed.

∽

Accountability enables a dream maker to set lofty goals with confidence they'll be reached, because a mentor will be standing at his or her side whenever he's needed.

It may be that the element of accountability causes you to dig in your heels. "I'm not going to let anyone police my life," you may insist. Or you may say, "I can make it alone."

If those two statements express your feelings, I'd suggest that you have an unhealthy view of accountability. Mentors don't serve as cops who hand us citations every time we fail to achieve a goal. They don't slap our hand with a ruler when we step out of line. Instead they provide us with the support and encouragement we need to achieve our potential.

Dream makers mentor in a way that nurtures and challenges, not in a way that controls and produces a fear of failure. Let me show you what I mean:[25]

HEALTHY ACCOUNTABILITY	UNHEALTHY CONTROLLING
Develops a relationship of encouragement, appreciation, responsibility. Focuses on the *process* of growth.	Seeks to control. Maintains lists of "shoulds" and "should nots." Focuses on behavior.
Guides, confronts, and affirms. Believes the best and nurtures a warm, relaxed, trusting relationship of mutual respect.	Punishes wrongdoing. Relationship stays superficial and task-driven.

I never would have seen the realization of my dreams in e-commerce without Bubba Pratt holding me accountable. His willingness to help me set lofty goals and then consistently monitor my progress provided me with indescribable incentive to give it my best. I love Bubba Pratt, and I didn't want to disappoint him. That kind of a relationship isn't developed without safety and trust.

Bubba believed I could make my dream come true, and he never stopped telling me, "You can win again, Joe."

I've got to admit that allowing someone else to serve as a mentor demands a humble, teachable spirit. As I mentioned before, when I asked Bubba, "Do you think I can succeed in the e-commerce business?" he said, "Yes, Joe. You can change."

Allowing someone to serve as a mentor requires a humble, teachable spirit.

Now remember, he wasn't talking to someone who hadn't already achieved a respectable level of success. But my success in traditional business didn't impress him. He knew that to succeed in a business that's relationally driven I would have to be *willing* to change the way I thought and acted. Not everything that worked in the world of trucking would work in the world of e-commerce. In spite of my past achievements, I approached Bubba Pratt as a rookie player would approach a seasoned coach.

If you're looking for a mentor, remember that nobody will mentor you if you think you've already got all the answers. Mentors want men and women with humble, teachable spirits who are eager to learn. And when they find that kind of a person—they'll provide him or her with the accountability he or she needs to bring his or her dream into reality. At the same time they're doing that, they'll make the final commitment.

Commitment #5: "When the time is right, I'll let you go so you can help others."

Every mentoring relationship starts with the end in view.

Nobody wants to serve as a mentor forever. Instead, mentors want to develop those under their charge so they can one day reproduce what they've learned in the life of another person.

Every mentoring relationship starts with the end in view.

I'm reminded of the story of a boy who found a sparrow in the woods behind his house. The bird didn't fly away as the boy approached because its left wing was broken. The boy took the bird home, made a cage for it out of sticks, and patiently nursed it back to health. It wasn't long before he came to love the little creature and began to think of it as his own.

Within a month or so the bird's wing healed. Soon it began to try to escape from the cage, flapping its wings and hurling itself against the bars. Seeing this, the boy's father said, "Son, you need to let it go. He'll never be happy in that cage. If you keep him, he'll only get hurt."

Finally, the boy agreed with his father and reluctantly took the bird out of the cage and carried it outside. Standing in his front yard, the boy continued to hold the bird.

"Open your hands," the boy's father said. "If you squeeze him tightly enough to prevent his escape, you'll hurt him. You might even kill him."

"But if I open my hands, he'll fly away!" cried the boy.

"Maybe so," answered the father. "On the other hand, if he flies away, you'll have the joy of knowing you enabled him to fly. Besides someday he may return."

The boy slowly opened his hand, and the bird flew away. He watched sadly as it flew away and felt a deep loneliness that persisted throughout the day. Early the next morning the boy was awakened by the sound of a bird chirping. He looked outside his window and saw a sparrow perched on the branch of a tree. He didn't know for sure if it was his bird, but as he went down to breakfast, he realized that his loneliness had gone as he thought about the sparrow flying from tree to tree, enjoying what it was created to do.

Mentors find joy, not in controlling, but in equipping. They celebrate, not that they mended someone's broken wing, but that they enabled him to fly. Dream makers know that without the help of a mentor they would never soar to success. And they know that once their dream becomes a reality, they have a responsibility to help others make their dreams come true. In the next chapter, you'll discover another lesson that will help you do just that.

DREAM MAKER SUMMARIES

- Learn from mentors so they can mentor others.
- Have a mentor who believes in them.
- Believe in those they mentor.
- Have a mentor who is dedicated to them.
- Dedicate themselves to those they mentor.
- Have a mentor who encourages them.
- Encourage those they mentor.
- Have a mentor who holds them accountable.
- Hold accountable those they mentor.
- Have a mentor who will release them when the time is right.
- Eagerly release those they mentor when the time is right.

GIVE PEOPLE SECURITY AND SIGNIFICANCE

*Dream makers take the blame for mistakes
and give away the credit for success.*

One hot summer day a small flock of ducks took up residence on the banks of a small pond in southeastern Canada. They hadn't been enjoying the clear blue water long before an outgoing frog struck up a conversation with one of them.

"How long will you be here?" the frog asked.

"Just for the summer," one of the ducks replied.

The friendship that started on that hot day in June grew into a close relationship. The frog and duck spent almost every waking moment together. At the end of September, when the days began to grow short and the leaves began to change color, the duck announced, "It's time for me to head south."

"South?" the frog inquired.

"That's right. It's time for me to fly south for the winter with the rest of the flock."

Clearly shaken by the news that he might never see his friend again, the frog said, "I wish I could go with you."

"Not possible," the duck replied, shaking his feathered head from side to side.

As the ducks prepared to take off, the frog had an idea. "Hey, I know how I can go with you," he insisted. Looking at his friend, he said, "If you held a stick in your beak, I could hold onto it with my mouth and in that way I could make the trip with you."

The two most important needs of every man, woman, and child are the needs for security and sifnificance.

"It would work better if two of us held the stick in our beaks," his feathered friend said. A few minutes later two of the ducks placed a stick between their beaks, the frog grabbed hold with his mouth, and they all took off for Florida.

After they had been flying for several hours, the flock of ducks passed over a farmer. He looked up and saw the frog hanging by his mouth. "Who thought of that?" he shouted loudly.

"I did," the frog exclaimed, widely opening his mouth.

Unlike that frog, dream makers know the value of giving away the credit for good ideas. They also realize the importance of taking the blame for bad ones.

Such an attitude is essential to success because it under-lines the value of every member of an organization or team. Nobody, I don't care how brilliant or talented he might be, ever brings a dream into reality alone. He must have the support of other people. And people most eagerly support a leader who creates safety by taking the blame for bad decisions. They also rally behind a leader who affirms their role by consistently giving away the credit for success.

Actually, such behavior isn't at all surprising. Psychologist Rallo May observed that the two most important needs of every man, woman, and child are the needs for security and significance.

A leader who takes the blame for mistakes provides security. One who gives away the credit for success provides significance. Dream makers work hard at creating an environment where people feel loved and important...secure and significant. Instead of opening their mouths and taking all the credit like the unfortunate frog, they point to the rest of the team.

While consistently giving people security and significance is a lofty goal, dream makers strive for it by putting into practice the four dream-maker laws of team building.

LAW ONE
PEOPLE FEEL SAFE WHEN FAILURE IS VIEWED AS THE PRICE OF THEIR EDUCATION.

"Today I'm pleased to introduce one of the most successful entrepreneurs in America." That's not a bad introduction, and the master of ceremonies meant every word. He wasn't just happy to introduce the guest speaker at the business luncheon; he was thrilled.

A large crowd of business leaders had gathered to hear Lowell "Bud" Paxson, speak. As the founder of the Home

Shopping Network and the father of PAX television, Bud had set himself apart as a brilliant entrepreneur.

"Well, I'm going to let you decide whether or not I'm a great entrepreneur," the six-foot-seven-inch tower of a man said. "I've started twenty-five businesses that I had to shut down because they didn't make enough money. I've had fifteen businesses that I sold for enough to make a little profit and cover the twenty-five unsuccessful efforts. And I've had two big winners."

After uttering those words, Paxson looked at the audience and said, "Now you tell me, how successful am I?"

He then noted that he had forty other stories that nobody had written about. These stories involved a fast-food franchise, an art gallery, a marketing company, and an electronic sign company.

There is no future in the past, and the past does not equal the future.

Paxson then drew the following conclusion, "I realize that each of those unsuccessful endeavors provided me with a lesson that strengthened my entrepreneurial skills. They made me a better dealmaker."[26]

Each of Bud's failures provided him with an education that enabled him to build the HSN and PAX television into successful endeavors. Dream makers create an atmosphere where nobody fears failure because they know failure is the price of an education. And nobody knows that better than dream makers. After all, they have their own list of failures. They realize that setbacks last only as long as a person allows them to last in his thinking. Setbacks are temporary, not permanent. Ultimately, dream makers know there is no future in the past, and the past does not equal the future. They commit themselves to learn and move on.

Not only have dream makers tasted the bitterness of failure; they've seen members of their team fail.

A $60,000 Education

Flying through life at a pace that would floor many people, Peter Legge picks up his adrenalin right out of the air and seems to get a revitalizing charge from simply being alive. Peter lives his dream as an internationally acclaimed professional speaker and as president of Canada Wide Magazines and Communications Ltd., a Vancouver-based publishing company with a healthy stable of fifteen magazines.

Soon after establishing his company, one of Legge's senior people made a mistake that cost the company $60,000 on the bottom line. At the time they were a small, growing company, and $60,000 was a lot of money. "Heck," Legge later said, "it's *still* a lot of money!"

Nothing creates security like the awareness that somebody else loves me enough to be at my side when I need him.

Legge had a serious talk with the executive about what happened, how it could have been avoided, and how vital it is to consider every angle when decisions of such consequence are being made. Obviously upset, the dejected executive handed Legge an envelope. Legge opened it and found the man's resignation.

A split second later he responded, "Resignation! You've gotta be kidding. I've just invested $60,000 in your *education!*

Get out of here and next time do better."[27]

In a sense, Legge shared the blame for the failure by acknowledging that the executive hadn't been adequately prepared for the situation he faced. Rather than tossing him aside like a used rag, he invested in his future success. Instead of treating failure as a job-ending event, Legge saw it as an opportunity for a key executive to learn some valuable lessons. No wonder Legge has seen his dreams come true—he practiced dreammaker law one and viewed failure as the price of an education. Why? Because he knows that a secure environment liberates people from fear and enables them to reach their potential.

Of course, there's the second dream-maker law of team building.

LAW TWO
THE MORE PEOPLE KNOW YOU LOVE THEM, THE SAFER THEY'LL FEEL.

Nothing creates security like the awareness that somebody else loves me enough to be at my side when I need him. One of the most powerful illustrations I've ever encountered involved the aftermath of the 1988 Armenian earthquake that killed more than 55,000 people.

Be there when you're needed.

Before the dust had settled from the earthquake, a father left his wife at home and raced to his son's school, where he discovered a pile of rubble where the school had once stood. As he gazed in horror at the scene, he remembered a promise he had made to his son: "No matter what, I'll always be there for you."

Tears streamed down his cheeks as he surveyed the debris that a few minutes before had been a school filled with laughing children. Finding his son seemed an impossible task, but he remembered his promise: "No matter what, I'll always be there for you." Because he frequently walked his son to school, he was able to identify the location that had once been his classroom.

With bare hands he began to throw aside the rubble. Others said, "It's too late; they're all dead; you can't help; there's nothing you can do; you'll make things worse; go home."

Without slowing down, he asked, "Are you going to help me?"

When firefighters tried to pull him away with warnings of possible explosions, he only said, "Are you going to help me?"

When the police came and told him that he was angry and distraught, he only said, "Are you going to help me?"

He dug alone for eight, twelve, twenty-four, thirty-six hours. And in the thirty-eighth hour, he lifted a boulder and heard his son's voice.

"Armand!" he shouted. "Is that you?"

"It's me, Dad. I told the other kids that if you were alive you'd save me, and that if you saved me, you would also save them. I told them about your promise, that no matter what, you would always be there for me. And you were, Dad, you were!"

"Are you okay?"

"There are fourteen of us left out of thirty-three. We're scared, hungry, and thirsty, but we're alive."

"Come on out, son."

"No, Dad, let the others come first. I know I'll be okay. You are here. You kept your promise."

When you consider your dream and the possibility of bringing it into reality, remember that you can't make it alone. And those who help bring your dream into being need to know you'll always be there for them. People eagerly rally around someone they know is always looking out for their best interests, even when the cost is high.[28]

LAW THREE
PEOPLE FEEL SAFE WHEN THEY'RE COACHED NOT CRITICIZED.

Being there when someone needs you may involve digging him or her out of a mess, but it also may involve using mistakes as opportunities for growth. While you want everyone on your team to view failure as the price of an education, you don't want him or her to miss out on the education.

My view on how to handle such situations is uncompromisingly positive. Scores of books have been written about how to offer "constructive" criticism. I've seen a lot more damage than good done with such criticism. When I see someone in need of growth (and who doesn't need to grow?), I view myself as a player-coach—somebody still in process.

A player-coach makes it clear that he's still learning.

One thing that helps me cultivate sensitivity is the realization that I'm still under construction. D. L. Moody was a great Christian evangelist who addressed massive crowds and founded several institutions. Despite his international fame and success he never treated others in a demeaning way. He used to say, "Right now I'm having so much trouble with D. L. Moody that I don't have time to find fault with the other fellow."

Dream makers never lose sight of the fact that they, too, are in process. And when it's time to coach someone else, they make sure the person they're coaching knows that as well. I do that with a technique I learned from my mentor Bubba Pratt.

A player-coach speaks in the third person.

Instead of pointing out the mistakes and shortcomings in others, I explain how Bubba handled me when he saw the same shortcoming in me.

If somebody's consistently late for appointments, I tell him, "You know, Bubba repeatedly told me how important it is to be punctual" (and he did).

If a member of my team isn't working diligently, I tell him how Bubba consistently urged me to work with diligence (and he did).

But I do more than coaching by speaking in the third person and sharing my learning experiences; I also like to tell a story that carries the message. As I'm doing that, I offer praise to every member of my team.

LAW FOUR
PEOPLE FEEL SIGNIFICANT WHEN THEY ARE AFFIRMED.

Everybody wants to know that his or her life matters. In fact, the more I get to know other people, and myself, the more I'm convinced that there's something people fear more than poverty, illness, or injury. In a sense, it's like our fear of death. We know that one day we'll die, but we don't think about dying all the time or we couldn't function. This fear is like that. It's there just under the surface of our consciousness. It's the fear that our lives won't matter. A fear that after we've lived and died life will go on as if we had never been there—just like a sand castle after a high tide washes it away.

Victor Frankl noted, "Clinics are crowded with people suffering from a new kind of neurosis, a sense of total and ultimate meaninglessness of life."

It's impossible to overemphasize the need people have to know that their life matters. That's why it's so crucial to remind people they've been created for an important purpose and possess the assets needed to fulfill that purpose. They need others to concentrate on something good in them and consistently lift that up! In other words, people need to hear words of affirmation that assure them their life is important—words that buoy their sense of significance. We must be balcony people for others.

You Would Fly Anywhere for This

When the great coach Vince Lombardi lay dying in a Washington hospital, Willie Davis came to visit him. Willie had been one of the greatest defensive ends who ever played. He had played for Lombardi during the glory days at Green Bay in the midsixties. Now he had come all the way from the West Coast to say goodbye to his old coach.

When Willie came out of the hospital room, several reporters greeted him. "Willie—Mr. Davis—why did you come?"

"None of your business!" he said under his breath as pushed past them.

The reporters followed him downstairs, where he waited for a cab. "Come on, Willie, tell us why you made the trip. You traveled across an entire continent to visit that man. Why?"

Most people would travel across America or around the world to spend time with some-one who could make them feel important.

Finally, a cab arrived and Willie climbed in without answering the reporters. As the cab pulled away from the curb, he rolled down the window, stuck his head out, and said, "That man made me feel important!"[29]

In a simple six-word sentence Willie Davis spoke volumes. Most people would travel across America or around the world to spend time with someone who could make them feel important. Dream makers never forget that inescapable truth. That's why they:

> Give the credit for success *to others*.
> Focus on the strengths *of others*.
> Value the viewpoint *of others*.

Dream makers consistently provide people with security and significance. Because they try to meet these two most fundamental human needs, they tend to bring out the best in others. In a sense, they use their skill and insight to lift up others.

Chopsticks at a Concert Hall

Dream makers do for others what a famous composer once did for a young boy. The nine-year-old had been dreading the evening for weeks. His mother insisted that he attend a big-time, formal piano concert with her. She hoped it would somehow motivate him to do what he'd resisted doing for years—practice the piano every day.

The antsy kid anticipated a night with high-society snobs dressed in tuxedos and long evening dresses. He couldn't imagine anything more boring than listening to grown-ups talk about their latest vacation or art purchase. And he dreaded hearing them comment on how much he'd grown since they last saw him. Did they think that maybe he should be getting shorter? Really?

He went, but not without digging in his heels. The concert hall was packed. The crowd had come to hear Ignance Jan Paderewsky, the world-famous composer, do his thing at the piano.

When the boy's mother turned to talk with friends, he decided to get out of his seat and get a closer look at the piano. As he approached the huge stage, which was flooded with lights, he was strangely drawn to the ebony grand Steinway and its tufted leather stool. Unnoticed by the sophisticated audience, he sat down at the stool, staring wide-eyed at the black and white keys. He placed his small, trembling fingers in the right location and began to play "Chopsticks." The roar of the crowd was hushed as thousands of frowning faces turned in his direction. Irritated and embarrassed, they began to shout:

"Get that boy away from there!"

"Who'd bring a kid like that in here?"

"Where are his parents?"

"Somebody stop him!"

Backstage, the master overheard the sounds out front and quickly realized what was happening. Hurriedly he grabbed his coat and rushed toward the stage. Without a word to the crowd, he stooped over the boy, reached around both sides, and began to improvise a countermelody to harmonize with and enhance the simple song. As the two of them played together, Pederewsky kept whispering in the boy's ear, "Keep going. Don't quit, son. Keep on playing...don't stop...don't quit."

Like that boy, every person on your team will face situations where he feels as inadequate as that boy did. His best efforts seem as out of place as "Chopsticks" in a concert hall. On those occasions he needs a dream maker to sit down beside him and provide the safety he needs to accomplish something beyond' himself...something that will give his life meaning. Someone who will tell him, "Just keep playing and your dreams will come true."

DREAM MAKER SUMMARIES

- Know that the most important needs of every man, woman, and child are the needs for security and significance.
- Help people feel safe by assuring them that failure is the price of an education.
- Help people feel safe by communicating that they need them.
- Help people feel safe by coaching them rather than criticizing them.
- Help people feel important by generously affirming them.
- Help people feel important by giving away the credit.
- Help people feel important by focusing on their strengths.
- Help people feel important by valuing their viewpoint.

AWAKEN THE DREAM
IN OTHERS

*Dream makers build momentum by awakening
the dream in others.*

Hidden in the tiny brain of a swallow is a dream that pulls it from South America to Southern California. Those delicate creatures fly twelve thousand round-trip miles, most of them over water.

Unlike a jumbo jet, they can't make the trip south or north without a break. So how do they do it? I've read that swallows carry a small twig in their beaks. When a bird tires, the twig becomes the "boat" on which it rests before resuming its journey. Amazing!

Before the trip begins, swallows spend the winter in Argentina. On precisely the right day at exactly the right time they begin their long journey north. I find it astounding that the birds arrive at Capistrano on the same date each year and stay throughout the summer.

I like that story because I believe those courageous birds are like most people. If you saw a swallow lighting on the branch of a tree in Argentina, you'd have no idea it would soon fly to California. From the outside it would look like most other small birds. But God placed something inside a swallow that magnetically pulls it to Capistrano.

Similarly, I believe that God placed a dream within every person. And I'm convinced that when that dream is awakened, people are capable of accomplishing seemingly impossible feats. Like a swallow, they'll overcome tremendous hardship to reach their dream.

If you're hoping to surround yourself with motivated people, it's crucial for you to learn how to awaken the dream in others.

Unfortunately, most people let their dreams hibernate. They get so caught up in living life that they forget that it ever captured their imagination. Years pass and eventually they don't even realize their dreams can be awakened. The greatest tragedy of their lives would not be failing in the pursuit of their dreams. It would be to live and die as though they never had dreams.

I'm convinced that one of my most important roles as a dream maker is awakening the dream in others. Notice I did *not* say, "Infecting others with *my dream*." Nor did I say, "*Placing* a dream within them." My desire is not to plant something foreign within another person. Instead, I want to enter the cave of his or her imagination and rouse from slumber the dream that's hibernating. I want to awaken *his* or *her* dream.

If you're hoping to surround yourself with motivated

people, it's crucial for you to learn how to awaken the dream in others. If you hope to activate an army of self-motivated people, then this chapter is crucial, because in it I'll show you the three steps I take to awaken the dream in others.

STEP ONE
DISCOVER THEIR DREAM

I've learned over the years never to presume that I know another person's dream. A number of years ago a reporter interviewed Marian Anderson and asked her to name the greatest moment in her life. The reporter probably expected her to mention the night Toscanini told her that hers was the finest voice of the century. Or maybe she would note the private concert she gave at the White House for the Roosevelts and for the king and queen of England. She might have been expected to say that it was the day she received the Bok Award as the person who had done the most for her hometown, Philadelphia. Most likely the reporter thought she would mention the Easter Sunday in Washington when she stood beneath the Lincoln statue and sang for a crowd of seventy-five thousand, which included Cabinet members, Supreme Court justices, and most members of Congress.

You see, had her dream been to sing before presidents, kings and queens, massive crowds, and dignitaries, then she would have mentioned one of those. But Marian Anderson didn't dream about such things. She said the greatest moment of her life was the day she went home and told her mother she wouldn't have to take in washing anymore.[30]

I suspect that if you had asked Marian Anderson what drove

her to practice so many countless hours, she would have spoken of her dream to provide her mother with financial freedom. Like that great vocalist, a person's dream may surprise you. Since that's the case, avoid projecting your dreams into his or her life.

Ask Questions

Instead, ask probing questions. Find out what he would be doing with his life if he had unlimited time and money.

Sometimes people are hesitant to talk openly about their dream. They're like Charlie Brown, who once asked Lucy if she had ever dreamed of having people call her by a special nickname.

"Have you?" she asked.

Charlie Brown said he had but would never reveal the name. After Lucy pleaded with him and promised never to tell anyone, Charlie Brown confessed, "I've always wanted to be called 'Speedy.'"

"You're kidding," Lucy said. "Speedy? Speedy Brown! What a joke!"

In the next caption, Lucy is seen rolling on her side laughing as Charlie Brown drops his head in dejection.

Assure Them of Your Interest

Many people are reluctant to share their dream because they fear how others will respond. Dream makers realize this and create an environment of safety by showing genuine interest and affirming the strengths of the person they're talking with. I like to ask people:

- "When you were young, what did you dream of doing when you grew up?"
- "What would you most like to be doing now?"
- "What would you most like to be doing in ten years?"
- "At the end of your life, how would you like to be remembered?"
- "What do you most want out of life?"

It's not uncommon for people to tell me, "I want to be rich."

If they say that, I ask them what they would do with their wealth. Often times that causes them to talk about the heart of what they'd really like to be doing with their life. Maybe they want to send their children to school, open a home for troubled kids (a friend shared that dream with me), generously support numerous ministries and charitable organizations, own a professional basketball team, take a world tour with their kids, or, like Marian Anderson, they may look forward to the day when their mother or father doesn't have to work any more.

When you're trying to discover somebody's dream, be patient.

When you're trying to discover somebody's dream, be patient. Avoid rushing him. This may prove to be one of the most important moments in his life (take a moment and contemplate that possibility). It's true because you may be the first person who ever asked him to put his dream into words. If you hear what he says and then quickly move on to another topic, you will invalidate the significance of his dream. Instead, dream with him. Help him visualize what his future might look like and celebrate the possibilities.

Once he has articulated his dream and begun to fill in the details, you'll know that his sleeping dream has come to life. The more he talks about it, the more his dream will awaken. As it rises from its slumber, you'll be ready to take the next step.

STEP TWO
DRIVE OUT THE DREAM ROBBERS

Dream robbers come in different shapes and sizes. The one thing they all have in common is their determination to undermine hope. Like the proverbial pack rat, they love to steal such valuable items as motivation, faith, and hope and replace them with cheap trinkets like negativism, laziness, indifference, and despair.

Dream robbers are masters of the quick-switch. Once they've entered somebody's mind, they'll try to convince the victim that they're actually a friend. They'll fill his mind with lies about how he never could have accomplished the dream anyway. They'll convince him that it's better to succeed at something that doesn't matter than fail at something big.

Once you've helped somebody awaken his dream, it's crucial for you to discover his dream robbers so you can drive them away. Once more, I can't emphasize the importance of this step. Here's why. You may meet with someone and see a change in his or her demeanor as he or she talks about his or her dream. A few days later you meet again and sense that the dream is gone.

It's not gone! Instead, a dream robber sneaked in and stole

his passion. He replaced belief in the dream with "realism." Your job is to expose the dream robber for the thief and enemy he is and help put a security system in place to guard the dream.

As a dream maker I've encountered a band of robbers you'll need to listen for. (Notice I said "listen for." You must probe to find out why the person you're talking with gave up on his dream and why he's reluctant to dream again.) It's crucial for you to be aware of these bandits and know how to deal with them.

Dream Robber One: "What will other people say?"

The first bandit whispers in a person's ear, "What will other people say?"

In light of that question, I have a question of my own. When somebody worries about what *other* people will think, is he worried about "balcony people" or "basement people"? I can assure you that he's not worried about the balcony people in his life. Why? Because balcony people give affirmation and support, not discouragement and despair.

You must probe to find out why the person you're talking with gave up on his dream and why he's reluctant to dream again.

How do you drive away this dream robber? Of course, if somebody has programmed his or her mind to repeatedly replay the voice of a discouraging parent or friend, it's hard to break the pattern. These are like audiotapes from that past that continually play in his or her mind, and most people don't know how to turn them off.

But you can break the pattern and turn off the tape by becoming a balcony person for him. While you're offering him words of encouragement, be sure to give him audiotapes and books so he can listen to others who will talk to him from the balcony. Introduce him to other dream makers who are learning how to ignore their basement people and focus on the words of their balcony people.

Dream Robber Two: Past Failures

Few robbers can steal incentive more quickly than the one who reminds a person about past failures. Like a hand squeezing his windpipe, this dream robber will drain all life from a dream by talking about past business, academic, relational, and financial failures. He'll destroy a dream by mentioning the disloyal friends who undermined his success in the past.

The past does not equal the future, and there is no future in the past.

When I find this dream robber trying to steal my incentive, or that of someone else, I review the stories of others who refused to allow past failures to steal their dream. Stories about people like Abraham Lincoln, who entered the Blackhawk War as a captain. By the end of the war he had been *demoted* to the rank of private. Over the course of his life Lincoln suffered two business failures and a nervous breakdown, and he was defeated in nine electoral races before being elected president of the United States.

Abraham Lincoln is regarded as one of the greatest leaders in our nation's history—but if he had allowed past failures to rob his dreams, we wouldn't remember him at all.

Never forget that Babe Ruth struck out 1,330 times. In between strikeouts he hit 714 home runs. R. H. Macy failed in retailing seven times before his store in New York City became a success. The list could go on and on. Few people achieve greatness on their first try. The vast majority of people who experience success do so because they refused to let past failures rob them of their dreams. As I noted before, the past does not equal the future, and there is no future in the past.

Dream Robber Three: Limitations

Dream robbers will fill a person's mind with all sorts of reasons why he can't make his dream come true. These crooks love to tell people, "You're not smart enough, fast enough, or strong enough. You don't have enough money. You don't know the right people." Such lies steal the dream from a man or woman's imagination as fast as you can say, "Where'd it go?"

> *"Dream big and dare to fail."*
>
> NORMAN VAUGHAN

When people begin to tell me about their limitations, I do two things. First, I point out their assets. Second, I tell them about other people who refused to allow their limitations to steal their dream.

For instance, on January 7, 1995, the *Vancouver Sun* ran a story about how Norman Vaughan had climbed a ten-thousand-foot mountain in Antarctica, less than five hundred miles from the South Pole.

Like me, upon hearing that story you might imagine Vaughan as a young, strong athlete. In fact, he was *eighty-nine years old*. Three days before the climb began, he celebrated his birthday by blasting off eighty-nine Fourth of July sparklers at the base camp.

The article began with a six-word quote from Vaughan that summed up his philosophy of life. "Dream big," he said, "and dare to fail."

The next time a dream robber tells somebody you know that he's too limited physically, emotionally, mentally, financially, or in any other way, tell him about Norman Vaughan.

I realize there are other dream robbers—in fact there are so many that an entire book could be written about how to recognize and defeat them. In most cases you can drive a dream robber away by focusing on the strengths of the person you're talking with, telling stories about other dream makers, and supporting him in his effort to make his dream come true. As you do that, you'll want to take the next step.

STEP THREE
DEVELOP THE DREAM

Once you've awakened the dream in somebody and driven away his dream robbers, you'll need to help him develop a strategy to bring the dream into reality. While there are countless ways you could do this, I've found e-commerce to be the most timely. I've generated a flow of residual income that is greater than I ever paid myself in salary when I owned one of the largest refrigerated trucking companies in the United States and employed two thousand people.

You may be thinking: *That's fine for you, Joe, but I could never do it.* If you said that, you're allowing a dream robber to steal your hope. What I've done could be done by anybody if he would seize the opportunity.

Suppose for a moment that the owner of the largest retail chain in the world approached you and said, "I'm going to give you a shopping mall that will be visited every day by millions of people." That news would be enough to make most people smile. But suppose this billionaire continued and said, "Furthermore, I'm going to stock every shelf with inventory. Plus, I'm going to have many big name stores—like, Sharper Image, Office Max, Toys 'R' Us, and others—occupy the mall."

What I've done could be done by anybody if he seizes the opportunity.

By now you may be wondering exactly how you would make any money at this mall. Sensing your curiosity, the retailer would continue, "Your mall will sell everything you presently buy at a price that's equal to or better than what you're now spending—and the products will be delivered to your front door."

"Okay," you say. "But how do I make money?"

The retailer smiles and says, "That's the good part. Every time you buy something you'll earn points, like frequent-flyer miles. At the end of every month you'll receive a check based on how much you spend at your mall."

"How will that enable me to make my dream come true?" you ask.

"Here's how it works," he says, still smiling. "If you like the products and the prices, you'll probably tell your friends. Every time you refer someone to the mall, and they refer someone to the mall, and they refer someone to the mall, you'll receive a check at the end of each month based on the volume generated by those in your referral line."

"Does this really work?" you ask.

At this point in the conversation you don't need to talk with the billionaire retailer anymore. Why? Because I can tell you it works. If you apply the principles you've found in this book to the business model I've noted above—you can make your dreams come true.

When Faust Chitty showed me this business plan, I had the wisdom to search it out and learn for myself whether or not it would work. Once I had validated the strength of the company, the character of those leading it, and the timing of the opportunity, I asked Bubba Pratt, "Do you think I could succeed at this new business?" And as you may remember, he said, "Joe, you can change."

If I could change and succeed, so can you. You, too, can become a dream maker. I share this example to show how I use e-commerce to help people achieve their dream. Whether you use this model or another one it's crucial to offer people a way to develop their dream…to bring it into reality.

THROW CAUTION TO THE WIND AND DREAM BIG

I began this book with lesson 1, which urged you to *throw caution to the wind and dream big*. I'd like to end it with one of my favorite stories about a young man who not only dreamed big, but also saw his dream come true.

During his senior year in high school, Monty Roberts handed in a seven-page paper describing his dream: He wanted to own a horse ranch. He wrote in detail about the ranch and even included a diagram of the two-hundred-acre ranch, which showed the location of all the buildings, the stables, and the track. He even included a drawing of the four-thousand-square-foot house that would sit on the dream ranch.

Monty looked forward to his teacher's response. Two days later the paper was returned with a large red F on the front page and a note asking Monty to meet with the teacher.

When they met, Monty wanted to know why he had been given a failing grade. "Your dream is unrealistic," the teacher said. "You have no money. You come from an itinerant family. You have no resources. Owning a horse ranch requires a lot of money. You have to buy the land. You have to pay for the original breeding stock, and later you'll have to pay large stud fees. There's no way you could ever do it."

After blasting Monty with these words the teacher continued, "If you will rewrite the paper with a more realistic goal, I will reconsider your grade."

Dejected, Monty carried the paper home and told his father what the teacher had told him. His father gazed into Monty's eyes and said, "Son, you have to make up you own mind on this. However, I think it is a very important decision for you."

After thinking about it for a week, Monty turned in the same paper without making a single change. He told the teacher, "You can keep the F, and I'll keep my dream."

Today Monty lives on a two-hundred-acre horse ranch with in a four-thousand-square-foot home. Why? Because one day he made up his mind to pursue his dream no matter what limitations he faced, setbacks he suffered, or barriers he encountered.[31]

Like Monty Roberts—each of us has to make up his or her own mind on this. As his father said, "I think it's a very important decision for you."

DREAM MAKER SUMMARIES

- Awaken the dream in others by asking them questions.
- Awaken the dream in others by assuring them of their interest.
- Drive out the dream robber who asks, "What will other people say?" by becoming a balcony person and providing audiotapes that offer encouragement.
- Drive out the dream robber of past failures by talking about others who overcame failure on the road to success.
- Drive out the dream robber of limitations by mentioning others, like Norman Vaughan, who didn't let their limitations hold them back.
- Develop the dream in others by showing them a way to make it come true.

LESSON ONE

"THROW CAUTION TO THE WIND AND DREAM BIG!"

Dream makers know that tomorrow's success is built on today's dreams.

- Dream makers throw caution to the wind and dream big.
- Dream makers possess transferable techniques that enable them to bring bodacious dreams into reality.
- Dream makers ask themselves, "What would I do with my life if money and time were not a problem?"
- Dream makers don't sit around waiting for their dreams to come true.
- Dream makers enjoy life because they do what they're passionate about doing.
- Dream makers have written out a life purpose statement that defines their dream.
- Dream makers dream in high-definition color and stereophonic sound.
- Dream makers would rather fail at attempting something great than succeed in mediocrity.

LESSON TWO

"DRAW A MAP FROM WHERE YOU ARE TO YOUR DREAM"

Dream makers know that reaching their dream requires a map.

- Dream makers know where they're headed and have a plan to get there.
- Dream makers have goals that are ambitious and achievable.
- Dream makers set goals that are measurable.
- Dream makers develop a strategy to strengthen their character.
- Dream makers develop a strategy to shape the world around them.
- Dream makers transfer their goals to daily to-do lists and diligently monitor them.
- Dream makers use their goals as a map to direct their lives and monitor their progress.

LESSON THREE

"DON'T TIPTOE INTO THE FUTURE— LEAP INTO IT!"

Dream makers see an exciting and compelling future and commit all their resources to its realization.

- Dream makers ruthlessly shed bad habits.
- Dream makers diligently cultivate productive habits.
- Dream makers manage their lives so that they make the best use of their time.
- Dream makers focus on the positive.
- Dream makers cultivate their faith in God because they know He is the source of their strength.

LESSON FOUR

"PURSUE YOUR DREAM WITH PASSION"

Dream makers see the future, and it fuels their emotional fires.

- Dream makers know that people are influenced more by their beliefs and emotions than logic.
- Dream makers know that enthusiasm is contagious.
- Dream makers know that everyone has a reservoir of enthusiasm waiting to be tapped.
- Dream makers cultivate enthusiasm within themselves by listening to the stories of other dream makers.
- Dream makers review their dream every morning and night.
- Dream makers build friendships with other dream makers.

LESSON FIVE

"WHEN THE TIDE IS HIGH—SET SAIL!"

Dream makers recognize strategic opportunities and seize them.

- Dream makers know that opportunities occur when the elements needed for their dream to be realized come together at the same time.
- Dream makers build the present on the future.
- Dream makers stay open to unexpected opportunities.
- Dream makers study opportunities to see if they're strategic.
- Dream makers talk with people who are riding the wave of success.
- Dream makers immediately seize strategic opportunities.

LESSON SIX

"GIVE AWAY LOVE"

Dream makers know that love is the glue that holds life together.

- Dream makers know the value of love and give it away.
- Dream makers accept people unconditionally.
- Dream makers know that everybody is a ten somewhere and diligently seek to find out where.
- Dream makers master the five love languages.
- Dream makers give words of affirmation to those who need them.
- Dream makers spend quality time with those who need it.
- Dream makers offer gifts to those who need them.
- Dream makers serve those who need to be served.
- Dream makers offer a pat on the back or hug to those who need it.
- Dream makers know that it's more blessed to give than receive.

LESSON SEVEN

"PERSEVERANCE LEADS TO SUCCESS"

*Dream makers know that their vision of the future
will only become reality through persistence.*

- Dream makers know that perseverance leads to success.
- Dream makes know that focus is the key to perseverance.
- Dream makers focus on their dream, not diversions.
- Dream makers focus on solutions, not setbacks.
- Dream makers focus on potential, not problems.
- Dream makers focus on their faith, not their failures.
- Dream makers repeatedly tell themselves: God + Me = Victory

LESSON EIGHT

"MASTER THE ART OF MENTORING"

*Dream makers learn from the success of others
and then pass the lessons along.*

- Dream makers learn from mentors so they can mentor others.
- Dream makers have a mentor who believes in them.
- Dream makers believe in those they mentor.
- Dream makers have a mentor who is dedicated to them.
- Dream makers dedicate themselves to those they mentor.
- Dream makers have a mentor who encourages them.
- Dream makers encourage those they mentor.
- Dream makers have a mentor who holds them accountable.
- Dream makers hold accountable those they mentor.
- Dream makers have a mentor who will release them when the time is right.
- Dream makers eagerly release those they mentor when the time is right.

LESSON NINE
GIVE PEOPLE SECURITY AND SIGNIFICANCE

*Dream makers take the blame for mistakes
and give away the credit for success.*

- Dream makers know that the most important needs of every man, woman, and child are the needs for security and significance.
- Dream makers help people feel safe by assuring them that failure is the price of an education.
- Dream makers help people feel safe by communicating that they need them.
- Dream makers help people feel safe by coaching them rather than criticizing them.
- Dream makers help people feel important by generously affirming them.
- Dream makers help people feel important by giving away the credit.
- Dream makers help people feel important by focusing on their strengths.
- Dream makers help people feel important by valuing their viewpoint.

LESSON TEN

AWAKEN THE DREAM IN OTHERS

*Dream makers build momentum by awakening
the dream in others.*

- Dream makers awaken the dream in others by asking them questions.
- Dream makers awaken the dream in others by assuring them of their interest.
- Dream makers drive out the dream robber who asks, "What will other people say?" by becoming a balcony person and providing audiotapes that offer encouragement.
- Dream makers drive out the dream robber of past failures by talking about others who overcame failure on the road to success.
- Dream makers drive out the dream robber of limitations by mentioning others, like Norman Vaughan, who didn't let their limitations hold them back.
- Dream makers develop the dream in others by showing them a way to make it come true.

1. Random House Webster's College Dictionary, s.v. "dreamer."

2. Lee Eisenberg, "Taking the Long, Sharp View," *Esquire* 100, no. 6 (1983): 305.

3. Adapted from Howard Hendricks and Chip MacGregor, "A Man Can't Just Sit Around," from *Stories for a Man's Heart,* compiled by Alice Gray (Sisters, Ore.: Multnomah Publishers, 1999), 97.

4. Adapted from Jack Cranfield and Mark Victor Hansen, "Another Check Mark on the List," from *Chicken Soup for the Soul* (Deerfield Beach, Fla.: Health Communications), 191–5.

5. Adapted from Ted Engstrom, *High Performance* (San Bernadino, Calif.: Here's Life Publishers, 1992), 226.

6. Jack Cranfield, Mark Victor Hansen, and Les Hewitt, *The Power of Focus* (Deerfield Beach, Fla.: Health Communications, Inc., 2000), 274.

7. Michael LeBoeuf, Ph.D., *How to Win Customers and Keep Them for Life* (New York: Berkley Publishing, 1989), 34–5.

8. Ibid., 35 (adapted).

9. Ibid., 36 (adapted).

10. Hal Butler, *Sports Heroes Who Wouldn't Quit* (New York: Simon and Shuster, 1973), 46.

11. Adapted from Sheila Murray Bethel, *Making a Difference* (New York: Berkley Publishing, 1990), 137.

12. Adapted from Curt Schleier, "Skating Champ Peggy Flemming" *Investor's Business Journal*, 4 October 1999, A4.

13. Harry S. Dent Jr., *The Roaring 2000s* (New York: Simon and Schuster, 1999), 29.

14. Ibid., 30.

15. Ibid., 31. This information is a summary found in Dent's book.

16. Ibid., 98.

17. The story of Gale Sayers and Brian Piccolo was adapted from Alan Loy McGinnis, *The Friendship Factor* (Minneapolis, Minn.: Augsburg Publishing, 1979), 40–1.

18. Ibid., 20–1.

19. The five love languages I discuss were drawn from Gary Chapman, *The Five Love Languages* (Chicago: Northfield Publishing, 1995).

20. Ibid., 14–6.

21. Adapted from "A Brother Like That," by Dan Clark found in *Chicken Soup for the Soul*, Jack Cranfield, Mark Victor Hansen (Deerfield Beach, Fla.: Health Communications; Inc., 1993), 25–6.

22. 1 Chronicles 4:9–10 from the *The Holy Bible*, New International Version (Grand Rapids, Mich.: Zondervan),1996.

23. Lee Iacocca with William Novak, *Iacocca: An Autobiography* (New York: Bantam Books, 1984), 34–5.

24. Joyce Landorf Heatherly, *Balcony People*, (Austin, Tex.: Balcony Publishing, 1984), 33–6.

25. I'm thankful to Rodney L. Cooper, Ph.D. for his helpful

insights in *Shoulder to Shoulder* (Grand Rapids, Mich.: Zondervan, 1997), 117.

26. Lowell "Bud" Paxson with Gary Templeton, *Threading the Needle* (New York: HarperCollins, 1998), 88–9.

27. Peter Legge, *It Begins with a Dream* (Burnaby, British Columbia: Eaglett Publishing, 1996), 69–70.

28. Ibid., 35–6.

29. Bill Glass and James E. McEachern, *Plan to Win* (Nashville, Tenn.: Word, 1984), 102.

30. McGinnis, *The Friendship Factor,* 30.

31. Cranfield and Hansen, *Chicken Soup for the Soul.*